The Black Revolt and Democratic Politics

The Black Revolt And Democratic Politics

Edited with an Introduction by
Sondra Silverman
City University of New York

D. C. Heath and Company
Lexington, Massachusetts

Contents

1 The Revolt Defined

JOHN B. TURNER AND WHITNEY M. YOUNG, JR.
Who Has the Revolution or Thoughts on the Second Reconstruction   1

HAROLD CRUSE
The Intellectuals and Force and Violence   10

2 Means To An End: Strategy And Tactics

BAYARD RUSTIN
From Protest to Politics: The Future of the Civil Rights Movement   14

STOKELY CARMICHAEL AND CHARLES V. HAMILTON
The Myths of Coalition   23

JAMES Q. WILSON
The Negro in Politics   26 ✔

CARL WITTMAN AND THOMAS HAYDEN
An Interracial Movement of the Poor?   40

GEORGE BREITMAN
How a Minority Can Change Society   53

3 Black Power: Significance And Prospects

CHARLES V. HAMILTON
An Advocate of Black Power Defines It   59

TOM KAHN
  Black Power: A Discussion   67

JULIUS HOBSON
  Black Power: Right or Left?   72

NATIONAL BLACK ECONOMIC DEVELOPMENT CONFERENCE
  The Black Manifesto   75

FRANZ FANON
  Reciprocal Bases of National Culture and the Fight for Freedom   79

ELDRIDGE CLEAVER
  Convalescence   81

4 The Revolt And Social Change

SONDRA SILVERMAN
  Epilogue: The Phenomenon of Ghetto Life   87

  Suggestions for Additional Reading   97

Introduction

The black revolt occurred within a cultural setting where the values of liberal democracy—of a pluralist, corporate state—have been considered a valid picture of the real social world. It is a setting complete with notions of freedom, equality, and the participation of citizens in the political processes, as well as with conceptions about the importance of success and the worthiness of material possessions. In this society, blacks could not arrive at the position commonly recognized as the sign of individual worth—cultural and material success. At a certain point in time, they asked, "Why?" What was the cause of the disparity between the American Dream and the American Reality as applied to blacks? Why could they not have their share of white affluence? The answer was seen in terms of white racism or white intransigence, the refusal to accord blacks the rights and privileges which they held to be due them. The black revolt was an active response to that answer

I

Individuals are born into a social system which has certain values, certain definitions of reality, which they as members of the community are expected to and usually do share. As newly-born or newly-arrived members, it is assumed that they will become socialized and will thus act on the belief that the system is legitimate and valid, that it is worthy of their acceptance. Most individuals do so by rote, assisted by communal institutions—the family, the school, the church, the mass media, the state itself —which inculcate common values.

Values, assumptions, and images of how things ought to work are both the outcomes of established norms of performance and the reinforcers of those same norms. The child knows what to do even if he does not know why he is doing it; the young boy knows how to act and will even be able to give reasons to support the value of such actions; the adult knows what role to play and what roles to expect others to play. By processes of socialization, the child learns what adult members of the society already know: what rules operate; what roles he is expected to play; what knowledge and skills he needs to play those roles. Children are taught how to behave in school, how to play with other children, how to eat their food, how to be skillful at certain games, how to speak the subtleties of the language, how to be proper and polite, how to observe the traditions of the society. They are instructed in the ideology of the political system and are taught to accept the forms through which that ideology is institutionalized.

Values, the life-blood of the system, make the system viable, for they succeed in giving approval to the means of organization and to the allocation of goods and services. They are the imbibers of character traits which, ideally, make the members of the system want to act as they are supposed to act, which make them play their assigned roles, live up to the society's expectation of them, and neither question nor reject their parts. Usually, individuals will act appropriately, for they have been socialized according to the accepted canons of behavior. They react automatically, obeying what they rarely question to be other than worthy of their respect. They orient their behavior to a set of precepts which have had meaning and consistency, to a set of unwritten obligations or unwritten rules which have worked in the past. They may act according to usage, custom, convention, or law, either because they find doing so convenient or advantageous, or out of fear of disapproval, social ostracism, or punishment. While a system must primarily depend upon willing acceptance of its values if it is to function on a day to day basis, there is always the coercive bank of force available to the state to demand compliance.

Where the values are unquestioned,

where they are taken as given and equated with reality, where there is genuine consensus about the "ought" and regular agreement between "ought" and "is," where the political organization (the government) agrees with the social organization (the community), people do what is expected of them, never posing questions of alternative patterns of behavior. Conflict arises when the assumed reality of the society—both the values themselves and the generally accepted reasons for supporting them—are questioned and rejected, when psychological or sociological conditions make for socialization processes which are incomplete or imperfect. Then, the image of how the society ought to be is at odds with the reality of how the society actually is. Tensions arise and expectations break down when the behavior of the individual or his group are out of kilter with the controls of the society, when an objective reality and a subjective assessment clash. At this point of strain, people either continue to accept assigned roles and activities although they no longer have an unswerving belief and undying faith in them, or they assign themselves to new, socially unacceptable roles. They question either the game, or the rules by which the game is to be played, or both.

Individuals no longer have confidence in the political authorities if they see values and reality in conflict. For having been taught one thing and having experienced another, they lose faith in one view of reality and orient themselves to a second. As a mode of expression, this reorientation may differ, running the extreme from alienation manifested as resignation to alienation manifested as activity oriented towards change. But in any case, the binding force of traditional values has been broken and is replaced by a new perception which demands commitment to a new order. The legitimacy of the regime is to be questioned and its capacity to reintegrate its dissident elements—to be responsive to their demands—is to be tested.

The movement for civil rights arose because of perceived inequities in American society between the reality of black life and a potential, normative alternative. The values, the economic arrangements, the personality expectations, the international environmental conditions pressured the Negro into a posture of rebellion against the accepted mores of the society. In a situation where the existing institutional structures could not meet the expectations of the blacks, where the established methods of action could no longer accommodate the events of the day, a protest movement arose and was sustained.

To say that activists began to make certain demands on the state and federal governments after the Supreme Court announced that state laws requiring segregation in the public schools were unconstitutional (1954) is not to imply that until then blacks and their white supporters were satisfied with the former's status in the society. Nor should it be taken to mean that until then they had refrained from using law suits, the ballot, or various political and economic pressures in the blacks' behalf. Throughout American history, there has been instances of black protest: slave revolts, plantation rebellions, protest conventions, the formation of black organizations to fight for civil rights, black nationalist movements, and mass protest marches. But after World War II, certain external and internal factors coalesced to make the blacks less content with small gains in the struggle for equal rights and to make the possibility of success in future fights more likely.

Among such factors we can cite briefly the following: the blow to the myth of white supremacy dealt by the Japanese; the emergence of colored nations in Asia and Africa with the demise of colonialism; the internationalization of domestic problems in the post-war era; the development of a national race situation into a foreign liability; the nullification of Southern legal norms of segregation by the Supreme Court; the emergence of a "Black Bourgeoisie" which conformed to the white middle class in attitudes, styles, standards of living, and aspirations, and which, because of their rising expectations as a result of increased urbanization, unionization, and growing educational, economic and political opportunities sought to break out of its social limbo and become part of white America. Against this picture of black improvement and white concern, stand other factors: the income and job disparities between whites and blacks; the failure of state governments to implement the Supreme Court's decisions in both letter and spirit, and the failure of the federal government to duly coerce the states; economic and physical reprisals against whites and blacks who were prepared to abide by the Court's decisions; the failure of either political party to be a spokesman for black demands.

In the South, the old social order was becoming obsolescent as a result of industrialization. The political system was operating on a set of feudal principles declared moribund by the processes of economic development and technological advances brought about in the post-Civil War period. In the Northern cities, where political machines had politicized ethnic groups trading favors for votes, blacks found little opportunity to repeat this pattern, given a matured economy. Urban political machines were both unable and unwilling to be the mobility vehicle for blacks as they had been for other ethnic groups.

To be black, for most, meant to be a victim of high prices and low wages, mismanaged ghettos, corruption, poverty, economic and technological change, unstable family life, psychological feelings of inferiority, rising yet frustrated expectations. It meant to be excluded from certain jobs and certain organizations and to lack the leadership necessary to assist one out of the bind.

To right these wrongs, to realign the "is" and the "ought" in matters of equality, a movement grew to correct the injusticies perpetrated on the blacks.[1] Forces were joined in an effort to reform matters in the name of equal rights—to reconstitute the reality in line with what activists had been taught that reality ought to be according to the charter values of the society.

[1] See the brief chronology of the civil rights movement on page xv.

In its fifteen or so years, the movement has experienced a series of transformations, both in respect to goals and tactics. What initially began as a middle class protest for racial integration in such areas as education, public accommodation, and voting changed into a more generalized revolt for improved living conditions for the mass of working class blacks. Events in Birmingham, the March on Washington, and the eruption of Northern ghettos forced whites to consider issues of economic equality based on conceptions of class as well as issues of social integration based on conceptions of race. In addition to wanting to free blacks from an inferior ethnic status, activists in the movement wanted to alter black "life chances"—educational opportunities, external living conditions, prospective earning capacity. It would no longer suffice to demand the elimination of explicit racial barriers which prevented blacks from enjoying those opportunities available to white Americans. It was time to put an end to ghettoization, to provide meaningful work outlets, to improve rat-infested houses owned by white slumlords, to get decent medical care, adequate welfare payments, meaningful education.

In tactical terms, litigation gave way to direct action, to picketing, boycotts, sit-ins, freedom rides, marches. The movement proceeded from legal action to political agitation to civil disobedience to violence—from persuasion to coercion, from a belief that gains could be made by peacefully persuading the majority to a conviction that gains would come only by threatening or actually disrupting the political and social routines of the country. The traditional ways of raising demands, along with the substantive policies of the political authorities, were now held to be immoral and unjust; and it mattered little if these had been sanctioned in official, formal terms by political majorities. With a loss of faith in the willingness or ability of the federal government to do what they thought it ought to do, many blacks reassessed the nature of the beast and concluded that violence was the only language which the authorities would hear and understand.

Favorable results—the meeting of black demands—were easier to achieve in the beginning. Sit-ins at lunch counters speeded up the timetable of integration: they prompted a rational analysis that in certain respects Jim Crow cost more than he was worth. But it was more difficult to dramatize the problems of the poor and to prove that American society would face a severe crisis should it fail to integrate the alienated rejects of the black slums into the mainstream of American life. In addition, solutions to ghetto problems were linked more directly to the American economic values of work and private property; as these, then, became the area of concern, the political direction of the movement was forced to change. It would require more than piecemeal mopping-up efforts to meet the dilemmas of ghetto life head-on, and these dilemmas were, in effect, microcosmic of the crisis of the cities and symptomatic of a more generalized rebellion against the prevailing values of industrial society.

Of late, the movement for civil rights has been transformed into activity directed towards creating black identity and black solidarity, towards consolidating sentiment, perceptions, and goals arising out of a shared black consciousness. In part, these developments are a new brand of ethnic politics. But for some few, there is now less concern with embracing the values of American democracy as formulated by whites, and more with redefining values and transforming the institutionalized structures through which whites are seen to have power. For these few, the cry moves from integration to separation, from achieving the materialism of a white culture to achieving what they perceive to be the humanism of a black culture.

Black Power, this new direction of the civil rights movement, is a complex of ethical precepts and tactical motions. As such, it involves more than a relationship between black leaders and the American government; it also includes notions of psychological equality and, bordering on Negritude, suggests that what is good for blacks will save America from its current state of moral decay.

In sum: we are concerned with the workings of American society, with the values geared to an industrial state, with the legitimating myths of a liberal, pluralist democracy, with the economic and political goals of achievement and equality, and with the roles played by actors seeking these imbibed ideals. In even more precise terms, we are concerned with the movement for civil rights within that society and against the background of that value structure. Blacks have said that they want equality, what whites have by virture of their being Americans but which they, the blacks, are denied because of the color of their skin. Most blacks have said that they want civil rights, the things which are bestowed upon American citizens *qua* citizens. They want to be included in the life of the nation, as they perceive it. They have an image of what rewards the political system distributes to white people, and they want to share in those same rewards. They want the same freedoms and securities which they imagine whites to have. They want the legal rights explicit in the Constitution: the right to free speech, press, religion and assembly; the right to due process of law; the right to equal protection of the laws. They want to vote and have a say in the political decision-making processes. They want the material rewards of the affluent society; they want the opportunity to make money and then to purchase what the society puts up for sale. Some blacks even want the potential of American society, a positive conception of the freedom to be free.

II

To realize the ideals and institutionalize the values of a democratic society, to bring the values in line with the structures which give them meaning, there must be rules for the decision-makers: who elects them; to whom are they responsible; how are they to be influenced and held accountable for their behavior?

Structures and channels must exist through which demands for altering the informal rules, formal laws, or government policy and personnel can be raised. Laws and customs must allow for the articulation of grievances by political movements, interest groups, or individuals to the political authorities who, by virtue of their legitimacy, are able to adjudicate among the conflicting demands made upon them.

Questions of strategy and tactics relate to one's conception of American society, both as to its substantive nature and its processes for social change. Is it an irrational, sick society in need of a total overhaul;[2] or a confused but basically humane set of arrangements in need of major or minor adjustments in different areas?[3] Is it a pluralist society?[4] or a hierarchically controlled industrial state?[5] Is power dispersed or centralized?[6] Are decisions negotiated by competing, organized interests, each committed to the democratic game, each acting as a break upon the other, each prepared to compromise, each sharing with the other a basic concern for the state's preservation, its general welfare, and its public interest?[7] Or, are decisions handed down from an elite group who define and supervise the game as they see fit?[8] Is Robert Dahl correct:

When one looks at American political institutions in their entirety and compares them with institutions in other democracies, what stands out as a salient feature is the extraordinary variety of opportunities these institutions provide for an organized minority to block, modify, or delay a policy which the minority opposes. . . . The multiplicity of check points that American political institutions provide organized minorities result from three inter-related factors. First, there is a great diversity of political institutions. Second, among these institutions there is no clear-cut hierarchy of legal and constitutional authority. Third, there is no *de facto* hierarchy of power.[9]

Or is C. Wright Mills:

. . . the political directorate, the corporate rich, and the ascendant military have come together as the power elite, and the expanded and centralized hierarchies which they head have encroached upon the old balances and have now relegated them to the middle levels of power. Now the balancing society is a conception that pertains accurately to the middle levels, and on that level the balance has become more often an affair of intrenched provincial and nationally irresponsible forces and demands than a center of power and national decision.[10]

Are blacks one of Dahl's competing groups? Or are they excluded from the democratic game? Or, even more to the point, does the game occur only at Mills' middle levels, after important decisions of war and peace have been made?

The conception which one has of power and power arrangements provides a mechanism for evaluating the black revolt. If power is to be seen in terms of the ability to authoritatively define values—of who formulates the fundamental principles of a social order—then debates will be over the validity of democratic capitalism. If power, on the other hand, is seen in terms of the ability to allocate goods, then debates will be over slices of pie, not over the pie itself. In the absence of ideological disputes, blacks will pursue their interest in slices;

[2] Herbert Marcuse, *One Dimensional Man: Studies in the Ideology of Advanced Industrial Society* (Boston: Beacon Press, 1964).

[3] Arnold S. Kaufman, The *Radical Liberal: New Man in American Politics* (New York: Atherton Press, 1968).

[4] Robert A. Dahl, *Pluralist Democracy in The United States: Conflict and Consent* (Chicago: Rand McNally and Company, 1967).

[5] C. Wright Mills, *The Power Elite* (New York: Oxford University Press, 1959).

[6] William Kornhauser, *The Politics of Mass Society* (New York: Free Press, 1959).

[7] David B. Truman, *The Governmental Process: Political Interests and Public Opinion* (New York: Alfred A. Knopf, 1951).

[8] Gabriel Kolko, *Wealth and Power in America: An Analysis of Social Class and Income Distribution* (New York: Frederick A. Praeger, 1962).

[9] Dahl, *op. cit.*, pp. 326–327.

[10] Mills, *op. cit.*, p. 296.

but to become one of the definers of life itself, blacks will have to aim (by means of their own choosing) at becoming part of the present or some future power structure.

In pluralist theory, change results from the negotiation of competing interests; in an elitist conceptual framework, it occurs because of a cultural redefinition on the part of an awakened or new elite. Pluralism lends itself to reform, for there are rules and regularized practices which exclude the use of violence (disorienting, coercive action), but which do allow for reasoned measures of social argumentation—the legitimate use of non-violent disputation as a method of persuasion. Elitism lends itself to revolution. The dichotomy can be seen by comparing, in the pages which follow, the argument of John B. Turner and Whitney M. Young with that of Harold Cruse: of "gaining full inclusion into society" as opposed to formulating "an anti-capitalist ideology." The idea of counterveiling power is intrinsic to arguments for coalition politics, be it Bayard Rustin's liberal-labor alliance or the pragmatic coalition of Stokely Carmichael and Charles V. Hamilton. James Q. Wilson points out the consequences of such coalitions for radical change, while Carl Wittman and Thomas Hayden, as well as George Breitman, are arguing for a series of structural reforms in the bases of power that would have the effect of radically altering the present set of institutional arrangements. Similarly, in the arguments for Black Power, we find pluralistic conceptions behind Hamilton's call for ethnic politics and Tom Kahn's assessment of Black Power as an integrative mechanism. Julius Hobson, writing from a Marxist perspective, finds Black Power to be the wrong approach, for it avoids the problem of meaningful change. But the last group of selections in this book, those from the National Black Economic Development Conference, Franz Fanon, and Eldridge Cleaver suggest, on the other hand, that Black Power has at least the *potential* of rejuvenating or redefining the quality of life in America.

There are problems attendant in the pluralist schema. First, pluralism assumes a discernable mediator of conflicts; but, in actuality, the decision-makers are not as readily identifiable on all issues as this model suggests they will be. And until they are, the problem of exerting the right amount of pressure at the appropriate spot remains a difficult one. To whom do you complain if you are black and are lacking in the skills to get you a good paying job in the industrial order? In addition, the more important the issue area, that is, the closer it is to the apex of values, the more guarded the decision-making jurisdiction. There are fewer avenues for exerting pressure as the problem moves from segregated seating arrangements in restaurants, to labor biases in the building trades industry, to quality education in the ghetto, to government expenditures for poverty programs, to foreign policy commitments.

Secondly, the argument is made that if there is disorder and chaos, no voices can be heard, no demands made except those at the end of a gun; however, if there is order and stability, all valid, informed and rational interests will get a fair hearing—an equal chance to compete for the rewards which the system has to offer. But neither American society nor the American political leadership is equally tolerant of all competing views. Outsiders, non-conformists, deviants of one sort or another, individuals who have been unable to make themselves over into the image of the successful American are not given an equal chance to play at the political game. This very intolerance of the "outs" and tolerance of the "ins" intensifies the existing alienation of the out-persons and out-groups. Paradoxically, American politics is tolerant of those who least need it, those who are already a part of the American mainstream, or those whose ideas are uncritical of the society's values and myths. Blacks, especially those who are unorganized or unemployed, because they feel that they are not getting their fair share of what the system has to offer, may look with distain upon the game of democracy and see the stability of the present system (a value for others) as not being in their own interests. Rejecting the existing system, they alienate themselves even further from mainstream America.

This brings us to a third point. If a group cannot get what it wants by playing according to the appropriate rules of the democratic game, should it not play according to some other set of rules? And where is allowance made for this in a theory which assumes the acceptance of certain ground rules? If a group considers its objectives valid and in its own interest, is it not better to achieve them by less respectable means than not to achieve them at all? Is the "critical" question, as Abe Fortas puts it, a question of method? Does the "survival" of our society as a democratic community depend on the procedures of the movement:

Procedure is the bone structure of a democratic society; and the quality of procedural standards which meet general acceptance—the quality of what is tolerable and permissible and acceptable conduct—determines the durability of the society and the survival possibilities of freedom within that society.[11]

Or is the case not that as stated by Herbert Marcuse:

Law and order are always and everywhere the law and order which protect the established hierarchy; it is nonsensical to invoke the absolute authority of this law and this order against those who suffer from it and struggle against it— not for personal advantage and revenge, but for their share of humanity. There is no other judge over them than the constituted authorities, the police, and their own conscience. If they use violence, they do not start a new chain of violence but try to break an established one. Since they will be punished, they know the risk, and when they are willing to take it, no third person, and least of all the educator and intellectual, has the

right to preach them abstention.[12]

The problem has its tension: necessary social change ill-arrived at or the continuation of the status-quo by accepting a set of appropriate rules for change. The choice is not an easy one; but we often fail to see it as even a choice, so geared is American society towards the rules of the "ins" and the forms of fair play.

In substantive terms, not all interests may be the same. And, so we may have to opt for substance over form, for those things which our individual consciences, at a particular moment, tell us ought to be the reality. The civil rights movement could argue that for equality to be realized, the rules of fair play had to be seen in perspective: as applying to the "ins" and as a potential device for delaying a more equitable distribution of the rewards of American society. The calm of oratory, of reasoned debate and persuasion, has to be contrasted with the violence of ghetto life, the covert force behind race relations, the inaccessibility of channels for democratic participation. If the American Dream was to be reestablished or established afresh, rules had to be utilized, adapted, or changed as seemed propitious. Abiding by rules may not be as preferred a value as equal rights, stability not as functional as disorder.

If the American Dream was to be realized for the blacks, unconventional and agitational methods, some of dubious legality, had to be used and force had to compensate for the lack of money and influence needed to wage more conventional and sophisticated lobbying campaigns. Private desires for self-improvement had to be linked to the publicized needs for general social change, and all of these were articulated through channels other than those traditionally accepted. For only then could the American dilemma be exposed for what it was, and only then could the argument be put

[11] Abe Fortas, *Concerning Dissent and Civil Disobedience* (New York: New American Library, 1968), pp. 60–61.

[12] Herbert Marcuse, "Repressive Tolerance," in Robert Paul Wolff *et al.*, *A Critique of Pure Tolerance* (Boston: Beacon Press, 1965), pp. 116–117.

for reactivating or restoring the values of a democratic society.

If Mills is correct, if interest groups exist to serve the interests of the elite, how is change possible? How are choices raised which are meaningfully different one from the other? How are alternative policies aired, mobilized around, and made the predominant victors? How is consciousness turned into policy? This is not the place, assuming that one possibly had the answers, to bare the blueprint for revolutionary change—be it by armed insurrection or political transformation. And there is also the grave question as to whether such change is even possible in advanced industrial society. But, nonetheless, there are intellectual obligations to spell out the implications of adopting Mills' interpretation.

First, there is a difference between changes which accept the rationale of the given society and those which reject that society. To be revolutionary is to move towards the power to define ultimate or charter values. Following André Gorz's distinction: "a non-reformist reform is determined not in terms of what can be, but what should be. . . . [I]t bases the possibility of attaining its objective on the implementation of fundamental political and economic changes. These changes can be sudden, just as they can be gradual. But in any case they assume a modification of the relations of power. . . ."[13]

Secondly, to be revolutionary is to recognize the need to create an alternative consciousness and then to place those with such consciousness into positions of social, economic, and political control. The prospects, for the betting man, are grim. But the potential for changing the game by refusing to play the game is there. It lies in those individuals who now feel themselves to be powerless in effecting political change given the existing situation, those who have lost faith in the rules of the game and who conceive of the political authorities as being bereft of legitimate status. But as with the reformers of the incremental model, they will have to examine a series of questions: what functions will conflict, social dislocation, and violence serve in their cause? What are the liabilities to be incurred from the use of legal or quasi-legal tactics? How is a moral position translated into a political program which, by definition, entails choice and compromise?

It is with these problems in mind—revolution or reform, qualitative or quantitative change, success or cooption—that the debate which follows is pitched.

[13] André Gorz, *A Strategy for Labor: A Radical Proposal,* trans. Martin A. Nicolaus and Victoria Ortiz (Boston: Beacon Press, 1967), pp. 7–8.

Chronology

1954   Supreme Court upholds enforced racial segregation in public education unconstitutional, *Brown* v. *Board of Education*

1955   Montgomery bus boycott

1957   Civil Rights Act of 1957
        Integration battle, Little Rock

1960   ⫟ Sit-ins
        Civil Rights Act of 1960

1961   Freedom Rides

1962   Albany, Georgia, demonstrations
        James Meredith admitted to the University of Mississippi

1963   Birmingham demonstrations
        Assassination of Medgar Evers
        Voter registration drive in the South
        Intensified demonstrations in Northern cities
        March on Washington

1964   Ratification of the XXIV Amendment to the Constitution, outlawing poll taxes in federal elections
        Freedom Summer
        Civil Rights Act of 1964
        ⫟ Riots in Northern cities
        Mississippi Freedom Democratic Party credentials fights at the Democratic convention
        Supreme Court upholds the Civil Rights Act of 1964, *Heart of Atlanta Motel Inc.* v. *United States, Katzenbach* v. *McClung*

1965   Assassination of Malcolm X
        Demonstrations in Selma
        Voting Rights Act of 1965
        ⫟ Riots in Watts

1966   Supreme Court upholds the Voting Rights Act of 1965, *South Carolina* v. *Katzenbach*
        Initiation of the Black Power movement
        ⫟ Riots in Northern cities

1967   ⫟ Riots in Newark and Detroit

1968   Assassination of Martin Luther King, Jr.
        ⫟ Riots in the wake of King's assassination
        Poor People's Campaign
        Riots in some cities
        Credential fights in Southern delegations at the Democratic convention

1969   Government, on state and federal levels, initiate investigations into militant campus and political black groups, in particular, Black Panther affiliates

Conflict Of Opinion

The Revolt Defined

"...*if* the civil rights struggle is indeed the current revolution in the United States, it is in many ways unique. At least until now the Negro has not been so much trying to change the American system as attempting to become a part of it. The greatest articulated concern is with just and fair access and with sharing in the rewards of the system. He is not directly seeking to put another class or another political group into power or control. He is concerned with change in those policies which exclude him, legally and extralegally; and he is concerned either with replacing those persons now in power who control such policies or with influencing them to change their exclusion practices and present pattern of reward distribution."

——John B. Turner and Whitney M. Young, Jr.

"People who call the Negro protest movement a black revolution do not really understand their own system, for a real social revolution in their country would involve a social dynamic of many correlated parts. Such a revolution would have very little in common with the foreign revolutions they have read about. It would amount to a massive social transformation of a kind unheard of before, and the elements for it already exist within the society either actively or latently."

——Harold Cruse

Means to an End: Strategy and Tactics

"We need allies. The future of the Negro struggle depends on whether the contradictions of this society can be resolved by a coalition of progressive forces which becomes the *effective* political majority in the United States."

——Bayard Rustin

"Viable coalitions ... stem from four preconditions: (a) the recognition by the parties involved of their respective self-interests; (b) the mutual belief that each party stands to benefit in terms of that self-interest from allying with the other or others; (c) the acceptance of the fact that each party has its own independent base of power and does not depend for ultimate decision-making on a force outside itself; and (d) the realization that the coalition deals with specific and identifiable—as opposed to general and vague—goals."

——Stokely Carmichael and Charles V. Hamilton

"The fact that many different alliances must be maintained will not only call for a high degree of tactical flexibility; it will probably also mean that the civil rights movement will remain divided and even at war with itself. The divisions among Negro leaders are the result not simply of personal rivalry or organized ideology, but of the effort to adapt a movement to

xvii

the necessity of simultaneously occupying incompatible positions in order to draw strength from others."

———James Q. Wilson

". . . the black ideology alone is incapable of leading to improvements in the everday living conditions of Negro people. It can be one vital way of stirring people into participation, but it cannot eliminate poverty. The elimination of poverty, we think, requires the mobilization of all the power of the 75 to 100 million Americans who suffer it or suffer over it."

———Carl Wittman and Thomas Hayden

"A minority, properly oriented and led, can go much farther than it has thus far gone to make the present system unworkable and intolerable."

———George Breitman

Black Power: Significance and Prospects

"Black Power must not be naive about the intentions of white decision-makers to yield anything without a struggle and a confrontation by organized power. Black people will gain only as much as they can win through their ability to organize independent bases of economic and political power—through boycotts, electoral activity, rent strikes, work stoppages, pressure-group bargaining."

———Charles V. Hamilton

"Obviously, some facets of 'Black Power' can be absorbed by this society; they conform with our tradition and value structure. In this category are the emphasis on self-help and the tacit acceptance of segregation. Other facets will be nominally accepted but really undermined. . . . Finally, there are elements of 'Black Power' that clearly cannot be absorbed. Whether one sees the ghetto uprisings as riots or rebellions, they will be stopped. The right to overthrow a government may be proclaimed by revolutionaries, but the right to suppress rebellion is claimed and, more importantly, exercised by governments."

———Tom Kahn

". . . given the same set of economic circumstances, a black slum lord will act exactly as the white slum lord acts. The black entrepreneur will be forced into perpetuating the system of exploitation if he operates as a capitalist. Black bankers will be dealing in the same money markets with their white counterparts and will thus be guided by the same rules of the banking game. In any system with primary property values, black policemen will protect black haves against black have nots."

———Julius Hobson

"We fully recognize that revolution in the United States and Africa, our Motherland, is more than a one-dimensional operation. It will require the total integration of the political, economic, and military components and therefore, we call upon all our brothers and sisters who have acquired training and expertise in the fields of engineering, electronics, research, community organization, physics, biology, chemistry, mathematics, medicine, military science and warfare to assist the National Black Economic Development Conference in the implementation of its program."

———National Black Economic Development Conference

"We believe that the conscious and organized undertaking by a colonized people to re-establish the sovereignty of that nation constitutes the most complete and obvious cultural manifestation that exists. . . . The struggle for freedom does not give back to the national culture its former value and shapes; this struggle which aims at a fundamentally different set of relations between men cannot leave intact either the form or the content of the people's culture. After the conflict there is not only the disappearance of colonialism but also the disappearance of the colonized man."

———Frantz Fanon

". . . the history of America in the years following the pivotal Supreme Court edict should be a record of the convalescence of the nation. And upon investigation we should be able to see the Omnipotent Administrators and Ultrafeminines grappling with their unfamiliar and alienated Bodies, and the Super-masculine Menials and Amazons attempting to acquire and assert a *mind of their own*. The record, I think, is clear and unequivocal. The bargain which seems to have been struck is that the whites have had to turn to the blacks for a clue on how to swing with the Body, while the blacks have had to turn to the whites for the secret of the Mind."

———Eldridge Cleaver

The Revolt and Social Change

". . . the black revolt has to be seen on two levels. First, its actions to date have been to demand an alteration in the rules and regulations of the democratic corporate state; second, it has the potential for calling into question the very values or legitimate ends of the civil or social order. On one level, it will bring about political reform; on another, cultural revolution. Lest we forget, there is a qualitative difference between the democratization of the political apparatus and a redefinition of what is good, true and beautiful—the consciousness of an alternative existence."

———Sondra Silverman

1 The Revolt Defined

WHO HAS THE REVOLUTION OR THOUGHTS ON THE

SECOND RECONSTRUCTION

John B. Turner and Whitney M. Young, Jr.

The civil rights movement has been variously defined—revolution, rebellion, revolt, uprising, disorders (creative or otherwise). Each term signifies a relationship of objectives to the institutions and values of the social order; each implies a different ordering of means to ends and a different understanding of social rules and political channels. In this selection, John B. Turner, Professor of Social Work at the School of Applied Sciences of Western Reserve University, and Whitney M. Young, Jr., Executive Director of the National Urban League, discuss their reasons for regarding the current upheavals among the blacks to be revolutionary in nature, a major break with the traditional pattern of white-black relations, and a call for fundamental changes within the black caste system. But, in line with the distinction between reform and revolution made in the Introduction to this reader, the authors do not urge a realtering of values but rather suggest a program to improve the blacks' position within the prevailing social system. Through the exercise of group power, *blacks are trying to integrate—become a part of the American system— by equalizing their status with that of other groups in American society. Here pluralist assumptions are retained, and, the democratic game is played by rule changes or the skillful use of present rules. Here also is ethnic politics: the use of ethnic identity (1) to organize politically, economically, and socially, (2) to enter into coalitions with allied interests, (3) to protect oneself against other groups, and (4) to achieve an equality of status with other groups.*

I. THE NEGRO AND THE REVOLUTIONS

The past twenty years have seen increased activity aimed toward improving the status of the Negro. This activity is characterized by some new inputs that distinguish these twenty years from those preceding World War II. Perhaps the most important new element is the greater predisposition of the Negro to assume risk in pressing for status equal to that of whites. A second has been the positive response of institutions, public

From *Daedalus*, XCIV (Fall 1965), pp. 1149–1163. Reprinted with permission of *Daedalus*, Journal of the American Academy of Arts and Sciences, Boston, Massachusetts. *The Negro American*, The Daedalust Library, Houghton Mifflin Company, 1965.

and private, which traditionally guard and promote our democratic and moral heritage. Perhaps a third is the still weak but yet impressive show of Negro solidarity and group discipline, which is at best a loose and shaky coalition.

There is a tendency both in literature and in conversation to refer to the current civil rights struggle as a *revolt* or a *revolution.* The label is a comforting one to those who have been concerned with civil rights for a long time, for at the simplest level *revolution* connotes an acceleration of pace. There is nothing automatic or magical, however, about the outcome of a revolution. Revolutions must be planned, must be led to the desired end. To achieve that end, evaluations must constantly be made to determine what is to be done. Therefore, those persons concerned with the management and stewardship of the civil rights struggle should be increasingly accurate in their use of this concept, and must constantly ask how the current civil rights thrust can in fact maintain its revolutionary purpose.

A revolution seeks change through "a sudden and violent break with the past." The temper of a revolution is "not tomorrow but now, not part of the way but all the way." Certainly the civil rights movement has conveyed this notion of urgency through its slogan, "Freedom Now." There is no denying that without the picketing, the sit-ins, the marches the nation would have progressed less rapidly, if at all, to its present position. The protests have provided a visible rallying point for *all* Americans, Negro and white, but especially for the Negro. They have become a source of pride, a builder of morale. Protests satisfy the need to take action to help oneself. When successfully designed, they provide a sense of tangible accomplishment. They have drawn the young and not-so-young intellectuals, Negro and white, who have participated in an effort to rediscover the full meaning of democracy in today's age of scientific discovery. But to what extent do the sit-ins, the lie-ins, the marches, and the other protest and defense activities promise, in the areas where they have occurred, a sustained

commitment to increase the pace of action to secure change?

Social revolutions seek change in one or all of the following areas: (1) in the locus of power and control, (2) in the rules of the game or in policy, and (3) in the distribution of rewards within the system for large segments of the population. It must be stated that *if* the civil rights struggle is indeed the current revolution in the United States, it is in many ways unique. At least until now the Negro has not been so much trying to change the American system as attempting to become a part of it. The greatest articulated concern is with just and fair access and with sharing in the rewards of the system. He is not directly seeking to put another class or another political group into power or control. He is concerned with change in those policies which exclude him, legally and extralegally; and he is concerned either with replacing those persons now in power who control such policies or with influencing them to change their exclusion practices and present pattern of reward distribution.

Realistically, though, the possibility of Negroes gaining full inclusion into society cannot be considered apart from other major domestic problems: During this era of unprecedented abundance and affluence, what is to be done with the one-fifth of the nation that is poor, with the second fifth that is economically deprived? Now that almost two-thirds of the nation lives in or near vast metropolitan complexes, what is to be done about the management and control of urban America, its obsolete housing, the increasing need for services, the archaic forms of local government and financing?

It is evident that, without viable solutions to these problems, any attempt to make the Negro part of the system will succeed only partially, thus leaving the Negro outside or forcing him to adopt a strategy to change the system. Viewed in this perspective, the nature and scope of the revolution is less clear, for the problems of automation and cybernation and of urbanization appear inexplicably entwined with that of Negroes being excluded from the main stream of society. If we are to adhere to the political and moral values of this nation, we cannot possibly progress in resolving one problem without making progress in resolving the others. Of course a certain amount of "slack" can be taken up in the system, but deeper and more permanent solutions will not be achieved.

Protest has been the Negroes' major weapon in the past and will continue to be a major part of the arsenal of strategies to win full participation. But the strategy of protest is not equally applicable in all situations.[1] As a means of bringing about a sustained step-up in pace it has a limited use. For one thing, it is easy to mistake protest for progress, to mistake tokenism—albeit tokenism on a broader basis than ever before—for a sign that reform or revolutionary ends have been achieved. In associating constantly with people who share our convictions, it is, in fact, easy to believe that the walls of exclusion have fallen; having won the opportunity to enter barbershops in one community, it is possible to conclude that barbershops in all communities are open, or, having integrated housing on one street, to think that the street will remain integrated forever. It is easy, having received newspaper, television, and radio coverage, talked with mayors and community leaders, sustained insults and suffered weariness during marches and picketing, to conclude that the revolution is ended. It is precisely this phenemenon that led Hannah Arendt to write in her study *On Revolution:*

There is perhaps nothing more detrimental to an understanding of revolution than the common assumption that the revolutionary process has come to an end when liberation is achieved and the turmoil and the violence, inherent in all wars of independence, has come to an end. This view is not news.[2]

A revolution is not a special moment in time. There is no such thing as instant revolution. Revolution consists of *before* and *after.* And we have yet to complete the *before.* Wisdom must be developed regarding its scope and the obstacles which it must overcome. Interim strategies and action must be planned to guide it to its intended outcome.

The reasons that, following the Emancipation, the Negro failed to dig in, failed to move more rapidly, are complex, yet as understandable as the slow strides now being made by the newly emerging independent countries of Africa. But to know why an action fails is not to correct it. Our situation today is much different from that of a century ago. In addition to the new inputs already indicated, there are other factors which might suggest a better climate for the efforts of the Negro: (1) Poor as the Negro's education is in comparison with that of whites, it is much better than it was a hundred years ago. (2) As a result of mobility and mass media, the Negro is more aware today of his opportunities, rights, and the discrepancies between his status and that prescribed by the moral and written law of the land. (3) The existence of large numbers of demoralized and alienated people poses a threat to an increasingly urban society. (4) The burden of the unresolved race problem weighs heavily upon the nation's effort to seek and maintain world leadership. All these contribute to the efforts of Negroes and whites to bring about a speedier solution to the race problem.

A hundred years ago the United States stood in the midst of another revolution. Although the Negro American was merely a pawn in that struggle, the expectations were that he would emerge a full participant in society. This he did not do. Most assuredly these expectations were unrealistic, but the warnings and lessons to be gained from the Reconstruction era cannot be ignored today.[3]

Nathaniel Weyl epitomizes the turbu-

[1] James Q. Wilson, "The Strategy of Protest: Problems of Negro Civic Action," *The Journal of Conflict Resolution,* Vol. 5, No. 3 (September 1961), pp. 291–303.
[2] Hannah Arendt, *On Revolution* (New York, 1963), p. 300.
[3] Nathaniel Weyl, *The Negro in American Civilization* (Washington, D.C., 1960), pp. 85–118.

lent years of Reconstruction in his view that no leadership worthy of the name emerged among the Negro masses to give them coherence, organization, direction, and goals. The Negro mass itself failed to meet the challenge of the new opportunities. During the hothouse period of Northern military protection the Negro failed to seize his opportunities. Weyl quotes James Ford Rhodes as saying that the fifteen Negroes who served in Congress "left no mark on the legislation of the time." It may well be that Mr. Weyl writes harshly, even unsympathetically, but the accuracy of his conclusions remains largely unchallengeable.

But even though the climate for the Negro's efforts has improved, there is much on the current scene that gives reason for intelligent concern. Within the larger society there is an increasingly visible resistance of the heretofore somewhat latent but hard core of white supremacy. Perhaps the newest acronym in the field of white supremacy is SPONGE, the Society to Prevent Only Negroes from Getting Everything. In a fashion not unlike that of the Reconstruction era the union of white supremacy and political opportunism can pulverize the economically and politically disorganized, the inept, and the naive. Once again, there is evidence of a return to violence to keep the Negro in his place —such violence was a major characteristic of the Reconstruction era.[4] The stiffening of resistance is to be expected. Prediction, however, is not enough; plans must be made to dissolve the resistance.

The larger society is also threatened by the economic and social problems already alluded to—namely, the impact of automation and cybernation upon the economic security of the Negro. Willhelm and Powell aptly phrase the issue in the question "Who Needs the Negro?"[5] Unfortunately, the laws and programs demanding that the employment structure be opened are being enforced at the precise moment when the requirements for entering and remaining in employment are being raised, and at a time when the preferences for manpower are shifting. The undereducated Negro is consequently placed at a disadvantage. Willhelm and Powell suggest that the real revolution is the economic one. They write:

As more of us become unnecessary—as human energy and thought themselves become increasingly unnecessary—the greater will be our social anxiety. Then perhaps we will become aware that racial strife today is not between black and white, but is instead a search for human rights in a world of machines that makes so many humans utterly dispensable.[6]

Within the Negro "group" there are also causes for concern; there is continuing evidence of political naiveté among the leaders and the masses. It is still extremely common to find Negro candidates for political office running in such numbers that they cancel out the chances that any one of them will be elected. Often the Negro electorate fails to support those elected officials who have risked their political lives to help the Negro cause. It is still frequently the case that the Negro electorate uses its vote primarily to veto rather than to seek remedial and corrective action.

At the moment there is danger that the efforts of the Negro to help himself may fall short of their target through over-dependence on protest action. As James Wilson points out in his article "Strategy of Protest," there are conditions which must be reasonably met if protest is to be successful.[7] When inappropriately used, protest fails to achieve the objective; this in turn lowers the readiness of potential supporters to participate. It can also mobilize the opposition prematurely. In a few instances,

[4] Maurice R. Davie, *Negroes in American Society* (New York, 1949).
[5] Sidney M. Willhelm and Edwin H. Powell, "Who Needs the Negro?" *Transaction*, Vol. 1, No. 6 (September–October 1964), pp. 3–6.

[6] *Ibid.*, p. 6.
[7] Wilson, *op. cit.*

as one might expect, protest is used to achieve purely individual objectives as opposed to group objectives. Such activity naturally creates doubt and suspicion among those who are called upon to participate; and it also undercuts the legitimacy of the protest in the minds of those against whom it is directed as well as among the general public. Ways must be found to protect legitimate protest from this abuse.

In summary, the current civil rights struggle is indeed revolutionary. First, it is revolutionary because it seeks and must find within the larger framework of social change a solution potentially involving modifications of traditional relations, between man and work and between man and his socio-political environment. Second, the civil rights struggle is revolutionary because, if it is to succeed, it must bring about rapid and radical changes within the Negro "group." These two revolutionary aims are not independent of each other. While it is clear that the major initiative and responsibility for the second belongs to the Negro, he cannot permit himself to become a pawn or onlooker in the broader revolutionary struggle. What strategy and what action is required of the Negro if the revolutions are to be successfully pursued?

II. THE REVOLUTION FROM WITHIN

Restating the problem operationally. In describing the racial problem many people confuse their definition of it with its solution. In other words, some people view the problem as the failure of the Negro to achieve integration, while others refer to it as the failure of the Negro to achieve an equal partnership in a pluralistic society. But the issue is incorrectly stated when put into these terms. It is dramatically clear, it is simple to describe, and it can be expressed in terms which do not confuse definition with solution. The Negro's problem arises because his minority status has brought about greatly limited life chances in comparison with those of the white majority. This disparity appears frozen in relation to the majority group.

In an address on civil rights to the Congress on February 28, 1963, the late President Kennedy stated this clearly. He said:

The Negro baby born in America today —regardless of the section or state in which he is born—has about one-half as much chance of completing high school as a white baby born in the same place on the same day, one-third as much chance of completing college, one-third as much chance of becoming a professional man, twice as much chance of becoming unemployed, about one-seventh as much chance of earning $10,000 a year, a life expectancy which is seven years less and the prospects of earning only half as much.

It is not necessary to detail these statistics further, for they are increasingly well known. In any area selected—economic security, citizenship, housing, education, family stability, health, crime —the Negro is subject to grossly unequal life chances. The effect is to reduce his opportunity seriously as compared with that of the white majority. At the same time it adds significantly to his burdens and handicaps as compared with those experienced by whites.

The equalization of life chances for all racial, ethnic, and religious minorities is not only a goal compatible with the values of our democratic system of government and way of life; it must, in fact, be realized if the idea of democracy is to remain viable for Americans. It is necessary if our system of government is to remain a model which Americans aspire to have respected and emulated in the world of nations.

To many people the solution to the problem of equalizing the life chances of the Negro is a simple one. If the Negro really wants to improve himself, it is up to him. If he is down and out, if he has fewer life chances, he has only himself to blame. People who see the cause of the Negro's problem as individual failure say to the Negro, "Learn to speak better, dress well but less conspicuously, become quieter and more moderate in your behavior, work harder, save your money, fix up your property, attend concerts and the symphony and ballet, visit art museums, frequent the theater, meet and know the right people, and your problems will be resolved. It will only be a matter of time. Haven't the Jews, the Irish, the Italians—even the Southern whites—solved their problems this way?" This prescription for solving the Negro racial problem is called acculturation or, more commonly, the "melting pot" approach. People who believe in this approach would seek to help the Negro equalize his life chances by making him a "dark white man."

This acculturation model has not solved the racial problem for two compelling reasons: (1) It is based upon the principle that, if a member of a sub-group can lose those characteristics which set it apart, he will become indistinguishable from the majority group and will thus have the same life chances as members of that majority group. This principle might work were it not for the Negro's skin color, which makes him an accessible target for group subordination and exploitation. (2) The "melting pot" approach is also based upon the principle that, if an individual can succeed in our occupational system, he can rise to the top of our status-hierarchy. But the Negro's efforts to develop economic security have come at a point in history when certain major changes in our economic system all but close the traditional doors to economic security. The day has passed when an enterprising small merchant can expand a pushcart operation into a chain of food, furniture, or department stores. The openness of the employment market is now controlled by a labor movement whose major concern is not the control of working conditions and wages but whether or not there will be enough jobs for its present members.

A strategy for action. If at this time Negroes cannot defend themselves as a group against exploitation by submerging their identity or by becoming indistinguishable from members of the majority group, they must prevent group exploitation by group counter-power. They must be able to deter and to ward off exploitation, to protect their group by creating conflict of interest between exploitative behavior and goals of equal or greater importance to the majority group.

The essential requisites for group-exploitation deterrence-capability are: (1) *power* or *ability* to cause others to act as one desires—even against their wishes if necessary, (2) *the will to use power* for group purposes, and (3) *the capacity to exercise power skillfully.*

The first task in action to equalize the life chances of the Negro as a group must be to mobilize power. There are many sources of power but three are particularly relevant for action—political organization, economic control, and group solidarity.

Operationally, political power constitutes the ability to elect officials, to pass or veto issues voted upon by the electorate, and to procure a reasonable distribution of the rewards of the political system. A prior condition for maximum political power is maximum registration and voter turn-out, disciplined use of the ballot, disciplined use of elected official influence, and the procurement of key jobs in the government.

Economic power means, operationally, the ability to withhold needed purchasing power, to influence vital centers of decision in regard to the allocation of economic resources, to mobilize capital for group interest, to control an equitable share of wealth, to get a fair return on the dollar spent, and to become dispersed throughout the occupational structure, with mobility in each occupational class. Essentially what is required is capacity to exploit economic opportunity and to apply economic sanctions. The Negro must engage in a program of economic development.

Group solidarity is perhaps the most difficult of the sources of power to define operationally. It means, in general, the capacity to mobilize psychological and social resources at the sub-group level. It is rooted in the mutual-help concept characteristic of many families where mother, father, brother, and sister sacrifice to some extent so that one member of the family may go to school, get eeded medical care, take a trip abroad, o into business, or seek some other amily approved and valued objective. t another level, people from the same eighborhood or city may pool resources o help newer members.

Group solidarity raises the question of roup identity, a difficult obstacle for the Negro because it was his identity (color) hat created his problem. This is particularly true when acculturation is the preferred method of solving the problem. But in employing exploitation deerrence as an interim strategy, group dentification is not only necessary but also more easily rationalized and accepted.

The question whether group identification is an end in itself or a means to an end will also arise. It seems to be clearly the latter, and its mobilization is justified on this ground alone. Whether t should become an end-goal will remain for future generations to determine. What *is* important is that Negroes should have the opportunity at some later date to make this choice.

The mobilization of power is not in itself sufficient for achieving effective action. As we have already seen, there must be the will to use it. The exercise of power is always at a cost, and the Negro group and its leaders must be willing to pay it. The Negro is caught in a vise between the pressure of American culture for individual success and the necessity for individual sacrifice if group success is to be achieved. Until this obstacle is understood and until Negro leaders and the masses place higher value upon group success, Negro group power can never be appropriately utilized for the ends of equalizing life chances. Every Negro institution, beginning with the family, must place high value upon cooperation in attaining group goals, while continuing to promote the idea of individual initiative. This is a complex and difficult assignment. The pattern of cooperation and collaboration must be visible and meaningful throughout the civil rights movement. It cannot be limited to a public facade of "togetherness." Civil rights leaders must be deeply committed to the value of mutual

aid as a means of accomplishing the common goal.

Collaborative action will not come automatically; it will be necessary to assign responsibility for its promotion. Nor will collaboration take place in a vacuum. It must take place around tangible, important objectives and, at first, around the more clearly achievable ones; for in learning to value highly cooperative endeavors "nothing succeeds like success."

Finally, power must be intelligently utilized. It cannot be wasted as if it exists in inexhaustible supply. It must be conserved, channeled into priority issues at the precise moment when it can do the most good. There are two major directions for action within which appropriate priorities must be set even though they will require periodic readjustment: efforts to change the rules of the game and efforts to help the Negro play a more skilled game within existing rules.

With respect to changing the rules of the game, the architects of the civil rights struggle must ask what policies, what programs, what practices at the national, state, and local levels are most crucial in equalizing the life chances of the Negro. There should be frequent and regular communication at the national level among the leaders and staffs of the major organizations in the civil rights field to determine the primary areas of policy concern. An elaboration of the prevalence, scope, and etiology of the gap between the life chances of the Negro and the white should specify the most important areas of policy change and policy development. Too often civil rights organizations have been satisfied with playing a monitoring or watchdog role. Such activity is undoubtedly needed, but alone it is an incomplete answer to the task at hand.

To an increasing extent, policy and program issues will not be clearly marked with the label of race. They are likely to deal with long-term plans for the social, economic, and political development of the community. To play a role in shaping such plans so that they do not work to his detriment, the Negro must become at least as knowledgeable about these issues as others are; and obviously it is to his advantage to become even more expert. Also, it will be increasingly important for the architects of the Negro's future to link minority goals to the goals of other interest groups such as labor, business, and religion and also to the goals of the commonwealth.

While community policy is being forged to alter the broad conditions which limit and control the status of the Negro, the individual Negro cannot stand aside and wait. He must make individual decisions within the limits of the present system to determine how best to cope with it. He needs motivation, knowledge, and skill to enable him to cope as effectively as possible with the complex of factors uniquely affecting him. Civil rights organizations must give serious consideration to programs designed to help the Negro deal with life as it is now.

There are two related ideas which should be a major part of such programs. First, the notion of excellence should be seriously reassessed and must become the test of social, economic, and political literacy. It is probably true that, in the past, the Negro has gained little advantage by excelling. Often incompetence became one way of retaliating against the oppressive forces in his life. While these explanations are understandable and were even functional to some degree, in today's society incompetence is highly dysfunctional. The idea of excellence must be disassociated from the idea of occupational status mobility. One need not become a teacher, physician, or judge to achieve excellence. Excellence is more than a demand for mere competence. It is a plea for the highest standards, and it is a plea for creativity.

In his book, *Excellence: Can we be equal and excellent too?* John Gardner points out that "the importance of competence as a condition of freedom has been widely ignored."[8] Opening the doors to opportunity—which is clearly a first condition—will not of itself bring about full participation of the Negro in society. The formula is much more likely to be opportunity plus contribution plus powe leads to fuller participation.

It is important that the Negro b identified among those considered to b the most skilled, creative, and qualified whether he be a garbage collector, house keeper, engineer, or politician. Some peo ple will ask why the Negro needs to b any more competent than anyone else The answer is simple: The Negro is no yet able to enjoy the democratic ano nymity of being anybody. Excellence will be one component in earning the distinction of being as good or as bad as anybody else. Now the Negro needs to concentrate on being at least as good as and better than most, if he can.

The second idea concerns the assertion or exercise of rights and opportunities. Civil rights programs must help the Negro take advantage of job, business, educational, cultural, social, and political opportunities in tangible ways. Freedom and opportunity must be used, or they wither away. What is needed is a massive on-the-job training program in socialization into society. Such a program should be close enough to the individual Negro that help can be individually tailored to provide a good base for continuing growth. It would demand a new approach to social education outside of the traditional setting, whether in schools or in social agencies.

Of major significance will be efforts to link the Negro middle class with the working class. This is badly needed by both groups. The dynamics of mobility are understandable, but the shaky connection at the present time is dysfunctional. Efforts should be made to strengthen this linkage. Programs designed to bring about social, economic, and political literacy cannot be fragmented efforts but must be built into the Negro organizational structure with the assurance that they can continue for several years.

There are two target groups in the Negro population that require special thought, study, and investment. These are *youth*—the next generation—and *men*. Ways must be found to effect a dramatic increase in our economic, social, cultural, and psychological investment in Negro youth. Likewise, ways

[8] John W. Gardner, *Excellence* (New York, 1961), p. 159.

ust be found to free the Negro male at very social level to assume responsibilty up to the limits of his talent. The ntire history of the treatment of the Negro is a travesty upon his masculinity. 'his travesty will not be easy to overome, but attention to Negro males hould rank high on any list of priorities. t should realistically adjust his selfmage upward.

There is need for a National Commision on Negro Youth which would pay pecial attention over the next twentyive years to the needs of Negro youth. The Commission should be a planning, esearch, and policy development operation. Its purpose should be to determine he direction and scope of programs designed to assist Negro youth in becomng full partners in the American system. It should seek to encourage and promote its goals through existing organizations, such as schools, churches, social agencies, certain public media, and to help bring into being new agencies where needed. Such a Commission should seek to sensitize all organizations having Negro youths as members to the need to assist them in overcoming the obstacles to full participation; to include emphases which strengthen the capacity of Negro youths to participate with equality in the larger society; to make use of the existing resources in carrying out these tasks. It is essential that special and combined resources be allocated to instruction, exposure, confidence building, and opportunity linkage.

Efforts must be made to widen public support for improving the quality and quantity of education in every public school district—obviously a first and necessary target. But, in addition, ways must be found to encourage the fullest exploitation of those programs which undergird and extend the work of public schools. Such efforts would not only involve institutionalizing present tutorial efforts for the undereducated, but would also provide a new approach to educative experience for the parents of these children, thus helping to create a more supportive environment in the home for education in general. Remedial and enrichment classes should be undertaken by such organizations as churches, labor unions, and social agencies. Instruction should focus upon full and responsible entry into the economic, political, and cultural activities of our society. These emphases will require that organizations rearrange their present patterns of allocations. Perhaps it will be necessary to offer inducements to organizations to change supplementary funding.

Role identification by contact and exposure remains one of the fundamental ways of motivating to learn. Negro youth are too frequently deprived of effective role models whom they can come to know in other than a superficial and vicarious manner. Youth need to become aware through first-hand experience of the reality of achievement, and to gain true perspective on costs and gains. Negro youth need systematic, repeated exposure—socially, vocationally, and physically—to effective role models as a major means of encouraging the development of their talents. A special fund should be established nationally to make it possible for several of the talented young Negro people in various fields to work and study with outstanding senior people for one or two years. Such a plan might even operate on a local level in some communities.

The theoretical ideas underlying the work of the President's Committee on Juvenile Delinquency and, more recently, the Anti-Poverty Program make clear the importance of actual access to opportunity. Instruction and exposure without opportunity will lead to bitter frustration and conflict. During the next twenty-five years even greater emphasis must be placed upon providing the Negro with truly equal opportunity.

Finally it is important that Negro youth be offered the opportunity to develop a sense of self-respect, worthiness, adequacy, and self-confidence as a human being. To the extent that the preceding conditions are met, self-esteem will grow. But an important additional input is his elders' belief in him, communicated repeatedly during the day-today routines of life.

As suggested previously, any serious efforts to help the Negro must take into account the needs of the Negro male, long denied his masculinity in a society which worships it. Reference is made here to two traits, aggressiveness and responsibility. (In the past, the Negro male has been punished for being aggressive and prevented from being responsible.) This history of castration has played a major role in the structure and dynamics of the Negro family. Certainly there are no panaceas and no substitutes for jobs. But, there must be an effort to rediscover and free the masculinity of the Negro male so that he can take full advantage of equal opportunity. Pilot projects are needed to help determine the most fruitful ways of accomplishing this goal.

In summary, the final section of this paper has suggested that the interim strategy for the civil rights struggle derives from a statement of the problem. The operational definition posed here focuses upon the gap between the life chances of the Negro and the white. It is suggested that where the "melting pot" response is prohibited as a means of defending against group exploitation, the alternative is to develop group-exploitation, deterrence-capability. The following elements are fundamental to group-exploitation deterrence: sources of power, will to use power for group ends, and skill, knowledge, and organization designed to change the rules of the system and to teach the Negro to play a more skilled game within the existing rules.

THE INTELLECTUALS AND FORCE AND VIOLENCE

Harold Cruse

The current civil rights struggles are rebellions; they will become a form of revolution only when they transcend their immediate objective—racial integration—and replace it with a set of meaningful, radical programs offering more than militant rhetoric, which in essence is but an attempt to "shoot" one's way into the capitalist system. Harold Cruse is a critic and writer, currently visiting Honors Lecturer at the University of Michigan and Acting Director of the University's Afro-American Studies Program. In this selection, he argues for a movement which centers around the economics of social change, one which relates the struggle for black rights to the altered nature of capitalism and that system's ability to contain and absorb those who are its critics. He decries the lack of programs calling for massive social transformation and the fact that the prevailing myths of democratic capitalism have not been rationally rejected.

As a prime victim of laissez-faire capitalism and its social imperatives, the Negro intellectual is pro-capitalistic in his every reflex. He does not see that the concepts of social equality for the entire Negro group, and unqualified capitalism, are contradictory and incompatible. The ideology of the Negro movement, in all its trends, protests against the *ill-effects* of capitalist society but *not*

From *The Crisis of The Negro Intellectual,* by Harold Cruse (New York: William Morrow and Company, 1967), pp. 367, 370–372, 379–380. Reprinted by permission of William Morrow and Company, Inc. Copyright 1967 by Harold Cruse.

against the society itself. This underlines the rational and organizational ability of the Negro movement and encourages the irrationality of nationalist anarchism and nihilism. It brings the Negro movement and all of its factions face to face with the hard social dynamics of American capitalism. This inner capitalistic dynamic, if left to its own momentum, subordinates and absorbs everything, including the Negro movement and its pro-capitalistic ideology. It can be no other way. As such, without an anti-capitalistic ideology, the Negro movement is doomed to be rolled back into submission. Nothing but welfare state politics and economics will be administered from above, in response to the lingering and sporadic Negro protests from below.

* * *

The American propaganda apparatus has created the great social myth that the Negro protest movement is, in fact, the Black Revolution in progress. This is stretching the word revolution to include anything from "pray ins" to the March on Washington. It is true that, to many whites, the very fact that so many Negroes are protesting all at one time in so many different places, is unsettling enough to induce certain opinion-molders to believe their own alarmist propaganda. Ghetto uprisings like Harlem and Watts lend credence to the spectre of revolution even more. But as long as these uprisings are sporadic, the American capitalistic welfare state will absorb them and, more than that, pay for the damage in the same way the government pays for the destruction caused by hurricanes and floods. Uprisings are merely another form of extreme protest action soon to be included under the heading of Natural Calamities.

People who call the Negro protest movement a black revolution do not really understand their own system, for a real social revolution in their country would involve a social dynamic of many correlated parts. Such a revolution would have very little in common with the foreign revolutions they have read about.

It would amount to a massive social transformation of a kind unheard of before, and the elements for it already exist within the society either actively or latently.

The Negro movement acts out its many-sided role under the influence of, and as a part of, the structural imperatives of the American system. This movement cannot function in any other way as its progresses from one stage to another. Its future failures or successes will depend on to what degree the movement succeeds (or fails) in mastering the imperatives of its own social dynamic. The more the Negro movement falls prey to the myths created by the system—that it is revolutionary when it is not—the longer will it take for this movement to create an advanced leadership. The more the movement absorbs the American myths, the more the American system will absorb the impetus and elements of the movement, and the more internal leadership disorientation will result.

Negro leadership generally functions, even during protest, with one foot out and the other foot inside the Establishment. Being neither "in," nor without hope of getting "in," Negro leadership encounters the difficulty of fighting and protesting against the very social system it wants to join. This means, in effect, that Negro leadership is not really fighting *against* the system, but against being *left out of it*. Therefore, what really worries the Establishment is not so much the cacophony of protest, but the problem of how to absorb the movement without too much stress and strain. The general staff of the capitalistic welfare state understands this situation much better than the muddled minds that run the civil rights movement. The administrative "brains" at the top of the American system may be pragmatically shallow, but not too shallow to understand that the Negro protest movement is not really a revolutionary movement, but rather a response to another kind of American revolution, the capitalistic revolution that threatens to alter social relations in the Southern states. Industrialization has driven Negroes off the farms and plantations into the urban centers; it has mechanized farms, built industries and increased trade. The Negro response to this process has been inspired both by rising expectations and the instability of being uprooted. If Negro leadership fails to understand both the complexities of this capitalistic dynamic and the potential power of the Afro-American social dynamic as an entity, then the entire movement is wide open to being absorbed and controlled by welfare state anti-poverty programs and their ilk.

If Negro leadership, especially the new young generation, also understood the history of the white Marxist Left, then they would better understand American capitalism and the Marxist Left's real position within it. They would see how the myth of the Negro revolution is used by both capitalism and the white Left. However, the inner dynamic of American capitalism has nullified any possibility of the Marxist Left leading a revolution according to its theories. Consequently, out of sheer political insolvency and desperation, the white Left swallows the myth of the Black Revolution and reads revolution into every actual or potential Negro uprising. The joke is that the leftwing buys its way into a pro-capitalistic movement on the hope that what the establishment calls a revolution, will in fact become one later on. But the white Left does not possess a single idea, tactic or strategy in its theoretical arsenal that can make the Negro protest movement a revolutionary one. All it can achieve is to intervene and foster such tactics as will get some persevering Negro activist leader jailed, framed, or exiled for utterly romantic reasons. As of now, the same capitalistic dynamic that absorbed and negated the white Left of the 1930's, has blunted the forward thrust of broad segments of the civil rights movement (including self-defense uprisings).

*   *   *

When Marxist leftwingers speak of the coming proletarian revolution (even in fancy), they know that according to the script, this projects something apoc lyptic in scope, a fundamental mass a sault on capitalistic property relation the abolition of the capitalist class i toto. But do they really believe thi now? If so, it is pointless to debate suc irrational beliefs. Yet, one must insist o asking—How can a social movemer that is demanding more and better job homes, education and other privileges— all of which are benefits that lie withi the social grasp of the lower- and th upper-middle-class frame of reference— be characterized as a movement that consciously seeking the abolition of ca italistic property relations at the sam time? Such a movement is not aime at overthrowing anything; although N groes want jobs, they want them *withi the existing economic framework*, fc the simple reason that Negroes actuall know no other kind of economic system real or imaginary.

Essentially, the Negro's outlook is de termined by the material conditions o the American capitalistic dynamic. Th Marxists would have to agree with thi assertion inasmuch as it corresponds t one of their prime postulates. Howevei it is also true that no foreign revolution ary ideology can really penetrate th Negro psychology, especially if it is anti capitalistic to the point of interferin with the desire to "make good" in th world. Moreover, American capitalisn is also able to offer the masses (anc even members of the intelligentsia large doses of spoon-fed socialism These fringe benefits of American capi talism—welfare relief, health insurance old-age benefits, anti-poverty programs etc.—are much higher in dollar value than the wages of many productive workers in the underdeveloped worlc whose countries are building anti-capi talistic socialism. Thus it is the heigh of romantic folly to believe that the American masses, of any color, coulc be motivated to revolutionary actions tc achieve something they already have in one degree or another. Whatever the American Negro has achieved economi cally, whether capitalistic or socialistic he has won under capitalistic condi tions. He will struggle for more only

ithin that framework—unless he is in-
uced otherwise through experience. So
ır, despite all the talk about the Black
evolution, he has not been educated
»r anything else. He is a child of the
:a of New Deal capitalism and all that
ıat economic philosophy implies. It will
take much more than the tactics of a
Robert Williams or the social analysis
of a Julian Mayfield to goad any future
Negro protest wave to attempt to "overthrow an entrenched political and economic power" of American capitalism,
either North or South.

2 Means To An End: Strategy And Tactics

FROM PROTEST TO POLITICS: THE FUTURE OF THE

CIVIL RIGHTS MOVEMENT

Bayard Rustin

Blacks constitute a mere eleven percent of the American populace. How, then, do they use their minority position to bring about a revolution or a series of reforms? How do they integrate into white America or separate out to form a black culture? In the selections which follow, Rustin argues for a liberal coalition, Carmichael and Hamilton for a pragmatic coalition, Wittmann and Hayden for a working class alliance. Wilson, in discussing the vote and conventional, orthodox politics, also exposes the problems and shortcomings of approaches based on coalition perspectives; while, from another view, Breitman elaborates upon the confining conditions of revolutionary change.

Bayard Rustin, Executive Director of the A. Philip Randolph Institute, argues that as the transition is made from a protest movement to a social and political one—from questions of civil rights to problems of social and economic conditions—the tactics employed must correspondingly change. Solutions, he believes, lie neither in moderate withdrawal nor in militant shock tactics, neither in acceptance nor destruction of the existing institutions. Solutions lie in programs of reconstruction, politically engineered through a coalition of progressive forces—the blacks, labor unions, liberal and religious organizations—who share common political objectives which could transform them, as the spearhead of a Democratic Party, into the country's consensual, liberal majority. Social justice is secured politically, he continues, not by a posture of moral abstention from the political foray but by the political linkages between community institutions and the existing power base.

I

The decade spanned by the 1954 Supreme Court decision on school desegregation and the Civil Rights Act of 1964 will undoubtedly be recorded as the period in which the legal foundations of racism in America were destroyed. To be sure, pockets of resistance remain; but it would be hard to quarrel with the assertion that the elabo-

From *Commentary*, XXXIX (February 1965), 25–31. Reprinted from *Commentary*, by permission; copyright © 1965 by the American Jewish Committee.

te legal structure of segregation and scrimination, particularly in relation public accommodations, has virtually llapsed. On the other hand, without aking light of the human sacrifices volved in the direct-action tactics (sit-s, freedom rides, and the rest) that ere so instrumental to this achievement, we must recognize that in deseg-gating public accommodations, we affcted institutions which are relatively eripheral both to the American socio-onomic order and to the fundamental nditions of life of the Negro people. a highly industrialized, 20th-century vilization we hit Jim Crow precisely here it was most anachronistic, dis-nsable, and vulnerable—in hotels, nch counters, terminals, libraries, vimming pools, and the like. For in ese forms, Jim Crow does impede the ow of commerce in the broadest sense: is a nuisance in a society on the move and on the make). Not surprisingly, erefore, it was the most mobility-con-ious and relatively liberated groups in e Negro community—lower-middle-ass college students—who launched e attack that brought down this im-osing but hollow structure.

The term "classical" appears espe-ally apt for this phase of the civil rights ovement. But in the few years that ave passed since the first flush of sit-ins, everal developments have taken place at have complicated matters enor-ously. One is the shifting focus of the ovement in the South, symbolized by irmingham; another is the spread of e revolution to the North; and the ird, common to the other two, is the xpansion of the movement's base in the egro community. To attempt to dis-ntangle these three strands is to do vio-nce to reality. David Danzig's percep-ve article, "The Meaning of Negro trategy,"[1] correctly saw in the Birming-am events the victory of the concept f collective struggle over individual chievement as the road to Negro free-om. And Birmingham remains the un-atched symbol of grass-roots protest

involving all strata of the black community. It was also in this most industrialized of Southern cities that the single-issue demands of the movement's classical stage gave way to the "package deal." No longer were Negroes satisfied with integrating lunch counters. They now sought advances in employment, housing, school integration, police protection, and so forth.

Thus, the movement in the South began to attack areas of discrimination which were not so remote from the Northern experience as were Jim Crow lunch counters. At the same time, the interrelationship of these apparently distinct areas became increasingly evident. What is the value of winning access to public accommodations for those who lack money to use them? The minute the movement faced this question, it was compelled to expand its vision beyond race relations to economic relations, including the role of education in modern society. And what also became clear is that all these interrelated problems, by their very nature, are not soluble by private, voluntary efforts but require government action—or politics. Already Southern demonstrators had recognized that the most effective way to strike at the police brutality they suffered from was by getting rid of the local sheriff—and that meant political action, which in turn meant, and still means, political action within the Democratic party where the only meaningful primary contests in the South are fought.

And so, in Mississippi, thanks largely to the leadership of Bob Moses, a turn toward political action has been taken. More than voter registration is involved here. A conscious bid for *political power* is being made, and in the course of that effort a tactical shift is being effected: direct-action techniques are being subordinated to a strategy calling for the building of community institutions or power bases. Clearly, the implications of this shift reach far beyond Mississippi. What began as a protest movement is being challenged to translate itself into a political movement. Is this the right course? And if it is, can the transformation be accomplished?

II

The very decade which has witnessed the decline of legal Jim Crow has also seen the rise of *de facto* segregation in our most fundamental socio-economic institutions. More Negroes are unemployed today than in 1954, and the unemployment gap between the races is wider. The median income of Negroes has dropped from 57 per cent to 54 per cent of that of whites. A higher percentage of Negro workers is now concentrated in jobs vulnerable to automation than was the case ten years ago. More Negroes attend *de facto* segregated schools today than when the Supreme Court handed down its famous decision; while school integration proceeds at a snail's pace in the South, the number of Northern schools with an excessive proportion of minority youth proliferates. And behind this is the continuing growth of racial slums, spreading over our central cities and trapping Negro youth in a milieu which, whatever its legal definition, sows an unimaginable demoralization.[2] Again, legal niceties aside, a resident of a racial ghetto lives in segregated housing, and more Negroes fall into this category than ever before.

These are the facts of life which generate frustration in the Negro community and challenge the civil rights movement. At issue, after all, is not *civil rights*, strictly speaking, but social and economic conditions. Last summer's riots were not race riots; they were outbursts of class aggression in a society where class and color definitions are converging disastrously. How can the (perhaps misnamed) civil rights movement deal with this problem?

Before trying to answer, let me first insist that the task of the movement is vastly complicated by the failure of

[2] The situation has worsened since Rustin's writing in 1965. Refer to some of the works cited in the Annotated Bibliography on this point, esp. Blau and Duncan, Ferman, National Advisory Commission on Civil Disorders, United States Department of Labor. [Editor's note.]

many whites of good will to understan the nature of our problem. There is widespread assumption that the remova of artificial racial barriers should resu in the automatic integration of the N gro into all aspects of American lif This myth is fostered by facile analogie with the experience of various ethni immigrant groups, particularly the Jew But the analogies with the Jews do nc hold for three simple but profound re; sons. First, Jews have a long history a a literate people, a resource which ha afforded them opportunities to advanc in the academic and professional world; to achieve intellectual status even in th midst of economic hardship, and t evolve sustaining value systems in th context of ghetto life. Negroes, for th greater part of their presence in thi country, were forbidden by law to rea or write. Second, Jews have a long hi; tory of family stability, the importanc of which in terms of aspiration an self-image is obvious. The Negro famil structure was totally destroyed by sla\ ery and with it the possibility of cultura transmission (the right of Negroes t marry and rear children is barely a cer tury old). Third, Jews are white an have the *option* of relinquishing thei cultural-religious identity, intermarry ing, passing, etc. Negroes, or at least th overwhelming majority of them, do nc have this option. There is also a fourth vulgar reason. If the Jewish and Negr communities are not comparable i terms of education, family structure and color, it is also true that their re spective economic roles bear little re semblance.

This matter of economic role bring us to the greater problem—the fact tha we are moving into an era in which th natural functioning of the market doe not by itself ensure every man with wil and ambition a place in the productiv process. The immigrant who came t this country during the late 19th an early 20th centuries entered a societ which was expanding territorially and or economically. It was then possible t start at the bottom, as an unskilled o semi-skilled worker, and move up th ladder, acquiring new skills along the way. Especially was this true when industrial unionism was burgeoning, giving new dignity and higher wages to organized workers. Today the situation has changed. We are not expanding territorially, the western frontier is settled, labor organizing has leveled off, our rate of economic growth has been stagnant for a decade. And we are in the midst of a technological revolution which is altering the fundamental structure of the labor force, destroying unskilled and semi-skilled jobs—jobs in which Negroes are disproportionately concentrated.

Whatever the pace of this technological revolution may be, the *direction* is clear: the lower rungs of the economic ladder are being lopped off. This means that an individual will no longer be able to start at the bottom and work his way up; he will have to start in the middle or on top, and hold on tight. It will not even be enough to have certain specific skills, for many skilled jobs are also vulnerable to automation. A broad educational background, permitting vocational adaptability and flexibility, seems more imperative than ever. We live in a society where, as Secretary of Labor Willard Wirtz puts it, machines have the equivalent of a high school diploma. Yet the average educational attainment of American Negroes is 8.2 years.

Negroes, of course, are not the only people being affected by these developments. It is reported that there are now 50 per cent fewer unskilled and semi-skilled jobs than there are high school dropouts. Almost one-third of the 26 million young people entering the labor market in the 1960's will be dropouts. But the percentage of Negro dropouts nationally is 57 per cent, and in New York City, among Negroes 25 years of age or over, it is 68 per cent. They are without a future.

To what extent can the kind of self-help campaign recently prescribed by Eric Hoffer in the *New York Times Magazine* cope with such a situation? I would advise those who think that self-help is the answer to familiarize themselves with the long history of such efforts in the Negro community, and to

consider why so many foundered on the shoals of ghetto life. It goes without saying that any effort to combat demoralization and apathy is desirable, but we must understand that demoralization in the Negro community is largely a common-sense response to an objective reality. Negro youths have no need of statistics to perceive, fairly accurately, what their odds are in American society. Indeed, from the point of view of motivation, some of the healthiest Negro youngsters I know are juvenile delinquents: vigorously pursuing the American Dream of material acquisition and status, yet finding the conventional means of attaining it blocked off, they do not yield to defeatism but resort to illegal (and often ingenious) methods. They are not alien to American culture. They are, in Gunnar Myrdal's phrase, "exaggerated Americans." To want a Cadillac is not unAmerican; to push a cart in the garment center is. If Negroes are to be persuaded that the conventional path (school, work, etc.) is superior, we had better provide evidence which is now sorely lacking. It is a double cruelty to harangue Negro youth about education and training when we do not know what jobs will be available for them. When a Negro youth can reasonably foresee a future free of slums, when the prospect of gainful employment is realistic, we will see motivation and self-help in abundant enough quantities.

Meanwhile, there is an ironic similarity between the self-help advocated by many liberals and the doctrines of the Black Muslims. Professional sociologists, psychiatrists, and social workers have expressed amazement at the Muslims' success in transforming prostitutes and dope addicts into respectable citizens. But every prostitute the Muslims convert to a model of Calvinist virtue is replaced by the ghetto with two more. Dedicated as they are to maintenance of the ghetto, the Muslims are powerless to affect substantial moral reform. So too with every other group or program which is not aimed at the destruction of slums, their causes and effects. Self-help efforts, directly or indirectly, must be geared to mobilizing people into power units capable of effecting social change. That is, their goal must be genuine self-help, not merely self-improvement. Obviously, where self-improvement activities succeed in imparting to their participants a feeling of some control over their environment, those involved may find their appetites for change whetted; they may move into the political arena.

III

Let me sum up what I have thus far been trying to say: the civil rights movement is evolving from a protest movement into a full-fledged *social movement* —an evolution calling its very name into question. It is now concerned not merely with removing the barriers to full *opportunity* but with achieving the fact of *equality*. From sit-ins and freedom rides we have gone into rent strikes, boycotts, community organization, and political action. As a consequence of this natural evolution, the Negro today finds himself stymied by obstacles of far greater magnitude than the legal barriers he was attacking before: automation, urban decay, *de facto* school segregation. These are problems which, while conditioned by Jim Crow, do not vanish upon its demise. They are more deeply rooted in our socio-economic order; they are the result of the total society's failure to meet not only the Negro's needs, but human needs generally.

These propositions have won increasing recognition and acceptance, but with a curious twist. They have formed the common premise of two apparently contradictory lines of thought which simultaneously nourish and antagonize each other. On the one hand, there is the reasoning of the New York *Times* moderate who says that the problems are so enormous and complicated that Negro militancy is a futile irritation, and that the need is for "intelligent moderation." Thus, during the first New York school boycott, the *Times* editorialized that Negro demands, while abstractly just, would necessitate massive reforms, the funds for which could not realistically be anticipated; therefore the just demands were also foolish demands and would only antagonize white people.

Moderates of this stripe are often correct in perceiving the difficulty or impossibility of racial progress in the context of present social and economic policies. But they accept the context as fixed. They ignore (or perhaps see all too well) the potentialities inherent in linking Negro demands to broader pressures for radical revision of existing policies. They apparently see nothing strange in the fact that in the last twenty-five years we have spent nearly a trillion dollars fighting or preparing for wars, yet throw up our hands before the need for overhauling our schools, clearing the slums, and really abolishing poverty. My quarrel with these moderates is that they do not even envision radical changes; their admonitions of moderation are, for all practical purposes, admonitions to the Negro to adjust to the status quo, and are therefore immoral.

The more effectively the moderates argue their case, the more they convince Negroes that American society will not or cannot be reorganized for full racial equality. Michael Harrington has said that a successful war on poverty might well require the expenditure of a $100 billion. Where, the Negro wonders, are the forces now in motion to compel such a commitment? If the voices of the moderates were raised in an insistence upon a reallocation of national resources at levels that could not be confused with tokenism (that is, if the moderates stopped being moderates), Negroes would have greater grounds for hope. Meanwhile, the Negro movement cannot escape a sense of isolation.

It is precisely this sense of isolation that gives rise to the second line of thought I want to examine—the tendency within the civil rights movement which, despite its militancy, pursues what I call a "no-win" policy. Sharing with many moderates a recognition of the magnitude of the obstacles to freedom, spokesmen for this tendency survey the American scene and find no forces prepared to move toward radical solutions. From this they conclude that the only viable strategy is shock; above all, the hypocrisy of white liberals must be exposed. These spokesmen are often described as the radicals of the move-

undermines radicals = Here & moderates

ment, but they are really its moralists. They seek to change white hearts—by traumatizing them. Frequently abetted by white self-flagellants, they may gleefully applaud (though not really agreeing with) Malcolm X because, while they admit he has no program, they think he can frighten white people into doing the right thing. To believe this, of course, you must be convinced, even if unconsciously, that at the core of the white man's heart lies a buried affection for Negroes—a proposition one may be permitted to doubt. But in any case, hearts are not relevant to the issue; neither racial affinities nor racial hostilities are rooted there. It is institutions—social, political, and economic institutions—which are the ultimate molders of collective sentiments. Let these institutions be reconstructed *today*, and let the ineluctable gradualism of history govern the formation of a new psychology.

My quarrel with the "no-win" tendency in the civil rights movement (and the reason I have so designated it) parallels my quarrel with the moderates outside the movement. As the latter lack the vision or will for fundamental change, the former lack a realistic strategy for achieving it. For such a strategy they substitute militancy. But militancy is a matter of posture and volume and not of effect.

I believe that the Negro's struggle for equality in America is essentially revolutionary. While most Negroes—in their hearts—unquestionably seek only to enjoy the fruits of American society as it now exists, their quest cannot *objectively* be satisfied within the framework of existing political and economic relations. The young Negro who would demonstrate his way into the labor market may be motivated by a thoroughly bourgeois ambition and thoroughly "capitalist" considerations, but he will end up having to favor a great expansion of the public sector of the economy. At any rate, that is the position the movement will be forced to take as it looks at the number of jobs being generated by the private economy, and if it is to remain true to the masses of Negroes.

The revolutionary character of the Negro's struggle is manifest in the fact that this struggle may have done more to democratize life for whites than for Negroes. Clearly, it was the sit-in movement of young Southern Negroes which, as it galvanized white students, banished the ugliest features of McCarthyism from the American campus and resurrected political debate. It was not until Negroes assaulted *de facto* school segregation in the urban centers that the issue of quality education for *all* children stirred into motion. Finally, it seems reasonably clear that the civil rights movement, directly and through the resurgence of social conscience it kindled, did more to initiate the war on poverty than any other single force.

It will be—it has been—argued that these by-products of the Negro struggle are not revolutionary. But the term revolutionary, as I am using it, does not connote violence; it refers to the qualitative transformation of fundamental institutions, more or less rapidly, to the point where the social and economic structure which they comprised can no longer be said to be the same. The Negro struggle has hardly run its course; and it will not stop moving until it has been utterly defeated or won substantial equality. But I fail to see how the movement can be victorious in the absence of radical programs for full employment, abolition of slums, the reconstruction of our educational system, new definitions of work and leisure. Adding up the cost of such programs, we can only conclude that we are talking about a refashioning of our political economy. It has been estimated, for example, that the price of replacing New York City's slums with public housing would be $17 billion. Again, a multi-billion dollar federal public-works program, dwarfing the currently proposed $2 billion program, is required to reabsorb unskilled and semi-skilled workers into the labor market—and this must be done if Negro workers in these categories are to be employed. "Preferential treatment" cannot help them.

I am not trying here to delineate a total program, only to suggest the scope of economic reforms which are most immediately related to the plight of the Negro community. One could speculate on their political implications—whether, for example, they do not indicate the obsolescence of state government and the superiority of regional structures as viable units of planning. Such speculations aside, it is clear that Negro needs cannot be satisfied unless we go beyond what has so far been placed on the agenda. How are these radical objectives to be achieved? The answer is simple, deceptively so: *through political power.*

There is a strong moralistic strain in the civil rights movement which would remind us that power corrupts, forgetting that the absence of power also corrupts. But this is not the view I want to debate here, for it is waning. Our problem is posed by those who accept the need for political power but do not understand the nature of the object and therefore lack sound strategies for achieving it; they tend to confuse political institutions with lunch counters.

A handful of Negroes, acting alone, could integrate a lunch counter by strategically locating their bodies so as *directly* to interrupt the operation of the proprietor's will; their numbers were relatively unimportant. In politics, however, such a confrontation is difficult because the interests involved are merely *represented.* In the execution of a political decision a direct confrontation may ensue (as when federal marshals escorted James Meredith into the University of Mississippi—to turn from an example of non-violent coercion to one of force backed up with the threat of violence). But in arriving at a political decision, numbers and organizations are crucial, especially for the economically disenfranchised. (Needless to say, I am assuming that the forms of political democracy exist in America, however imperfectly, that they are valued, and that elitist or putschist conceptions of exercising power are beyond the pale of discussion for the civil rights movement.)

Neither that movement nor the country's twenty million black people can win political power alone. We need allies. The future of the Negro struggle depends on whether the contradictions of this society can be resolved by a coalition

of progressive forces which becomes the *effective* political majority in the United States. I speak of the coalition which staged the March on Washington, passed the Civil Rights Act, and laid the basis for the Johnson landslide—Negroes, trade unionists, liberals, and religious groups.

There are those who argue that a coalition strategy would force the Negro to surrender his political independence to white liberals, that he would be neutralized, deprived of his cutting edge, absorbed into the Establishment. Some who take this position urged last year that votes be withheld from the Johnson-Humphrey ticket as a demonstration of the Negro's political power. Curiously enough, these people who sought to demonstrate power through the non-exercise of it, also point to the Negro "swing vote" in crucial urban areas as the source of the Negro's independent political power. But here they are closer to being right: the urban Negro vote will grow in importance in the coming years. If there is anything positive in the spread of the ghetto, it is the potential political power base thus created, and to realize this potential is one of the most challenging and urgent tasks before the civil rights movement. If the movement can wrest leadership of the ghetto vote from the machines, it will have acquired an organized constituency such as other major groups in our society now have.

But we must also remember that the effectiveness of a swing vote depends solely on "other" votes. It derives its power from them. In that sense, it can never be "independent," but must opt for one candidate or the other, even if by default. Thus coalitions are inescapable, however tentative they may be. And this is the case in all but those few situations in which Negroes running on an independent ticket might conceivably win. "Independence," in other words, is not a value in itself. The issue is which coalition to join and how to make it responsive to your program. Necessarily there will be compromise. But the difference between expediency and morality in politics is the difference between sell-ng out a principle and making smaller concessions to win larger ones. The leader who shrinks from this task reveals not his purity but his lack of political sense.

The task of molding a political movement out of the March on Washington coalition is not simple, but no alternatives have been advanced. We need to choose our allies on the basis of common political objectives. It has become fashionable in some no-win Negro circles to decry the white liberal as the main enemy (his hypocrisy is what sustains racism); by virtue of this reverse recitation of the reactionary's litany (liberalism leads to socialism, which leads to Communism) the Negro is left in majestic isolation, except for a tiny band of fervent white initiates. But the objective fact is that *Eastland and Goldwater* are the main enemies—they and the opponents of civil rights, of the war on poverty, of medicare, of social security, of federal aid to education, of unions, and so forth. The labor movement, despite its obvious faults, has been the largest single organized force in this country pushing for progressive social legislation. And where the Negro-labor-liberal axis is weak, as in the farm belt, it was the religious groups that were most influential in rallying support for the Civil Rights Bill.

The durability of the coalition was interestingly tested during the election. I do not believe that the Johnson landslide proved the "white backlash" to be a myth. It proved, rather, that economic interests are more fundamental than prejudice: the backlashers decided that loss of social security was, after all, too high a price to pay for a slap at the Negro. This lesson was a valuable first step in re-educating such people, and it must be kept alive, for the civil rights movement will be advanced only to the degree that social and economic welfare gets to be inextricably entangled with civil rights.

The 1964 elections marked a turning point in American politics. The Democratic landslide was not merely the result of a negative reaction to Goldwaterism; it was also the expression of a majority liberal consensus. The near unanimity with which Negro voters joined in that expression[3] was, I am convinced, a vindication of the July 25th statement by Negro leaders calling for a strategic turn toward political action and a temporary curtailment of mass demonstrations. Despite the contraversy surrounding the statement, the instinctive response it met with in the community is suggested by the fact that demonstrations were down 75 per cent as compared with the same period in 1963. But should so high a percentage of Negro voters have gone to Johnson, or should they have held back to narrow his margin of victory and thus give greater visibility to our swing vote? How has our loyalty changed things? Certainly the Negro vote had higher visibility in 1960, when a switch of only 7 per cent from the Republican column of 1956 elected President Kennedy. But the slimness of Kennedy's victory—of his "mandate"—dictated a go-slow approach on civil rights, at least until the Birmingham upheaval.

Although Johnson's popular majority was so large that he could have won without such overwhelming Negro support, that support was important from several angles. Beyond adding to Johnson's total national margin, it was specifically responsible for his victories in Virginia, Florida, Tennessee, and Arkansas. Goldwater took only those states where fewer than 45 per cent of eligible Negroes were registered. That Johnson would have won those states had Negro voting rights been enforced is a lesson not likely to be lost on a man who would have been happy with a unanimous electoral college. In any case, the 1.6 million Southern Negroes who voted have had a shattering impact on the Southern political party structure, as illustrated in the changed composition of the Southern congressional delegation. The "backlash" gave the Republicans five House seats in Alabama, one in Georgia, and one in Mississippi. But on the Democratic side, seven segregationists were defeated while all nine Southerners who

[3] Cf. the Negroes' continued support for Humphrey in the 1968 Presidential election. [Editor's note.]

voted for the Civil Rights Act were re-elected. It may be premature to predict a Southern Democratic party of Negroes and white moderates and a Republican Party of refugee racists and economic conservatives, but there certainly is a strong tendency toward such a realignment; and an additional 3.6 million Negroes of voting age in the eleven Southern states are still to be heard from. Even the *tendency* toward disintegration of the Democratic party's racist wing defines a new context for Presidential and liberal strategy in the congressional battles ahead. Thus the Negro vote (North as well as South), while not *decisive* in the Presidential race, was enormously effective. It was a dramatic element of a historic mandate which contains vast possibilities and dangers that will fundamentally affect the future course of the civil rights movement.

The liberal congressional sweep raises hope for an assault on the seniority system, Rule Twenty-two, and other citadels of Dixiecrat-Republican power. The overwhelming of this conservative coalition should also mean progress on much bottlenecked legislation of profound interest to the movement (e.g., bills by Senators Clark and Nelson on planning, manpower, and employment). Moreover, the irrelevance of the South to Johnson's victory gives the President more freedom to act than his predecessor had and more leverage to the movement to pressure for executive action in Mississippi and other racist strongholds.

None of this *guarantees* vigorous executive or legislative action, for the other side of the Johnson landslide is that it has a Gaullist quality. Goldwater's capture of the Republican party forced into the Democratic camp many disparate elements which do not belong there, Big Business being the major example. Johnson, who wants to be President "of all people," may try to keep his new coalition together by sticking close to the political center. But if he decides to do this, it is unlikely that even his political genius will be able to hold together a coalition so inherently unstable and rife with contradictions. It must come apart. Should it do so while Johnson is pursu-

ing a centrist course, then the mandate will have been wastefully dissipated. However, if the mandate is seized upon to set fundamental changes in motion, then the basis can be laid for a new mandate, a new coalition including hitherto inert and dispossed strata of the population.

Here is where the cutting edge of the civil rights movement can be applied. We must see to it that the reorganization of the "consensus party" proceeds along lines which will make it an effective vehicle for social reconstruction, a role it cannot play so long as it furnishes Southern racism with its national political power. (One of Barry Goldwater's few attractive ideas was that the Dixiecrats belong with him in the same party.) And nowhere has the civil rights movement's political cutting edge been more magnificently demonstrated than at Atlantic City, where the Mississippi Freedom Democratic Party not only secured recognition as a bona fide component of the national party, but in the process routed the representatives of the most rabid racists—the white Mississippi and Alabama delegations.[4] While I still believe that the FDP made a tactical error in spurning the compromise, there is no question that they launched a political revolution whose logic is the displacement of Dixiecrat power. They launched that revolution within a major political institution and as part of a coalitional effort.

The role of the civil rights movement in the reorganization of American political life is programmatic as well as strategic. We are challenged now to broaden our social vision, to develop functional programs with concrete objectives. We need to propose alternatives to technological unemployment, urban decay, and the rest. We need to be calling for public works and training, for national economic planning, for federal aid to education, for attractive public housing—all this on a sufficiently massive scale to make a difference. We need to protest the notion that our integration into American life, so long delayed, must

[4] Similar moves were made and similar victories won in the 1968 convention. [Editor's note.]

now proceed in an atmosphere of competitive scarcity instead of in the security of abundance which technology makes possible. We cannot claim to have answers to all the complex problems of modern society. That is too much to ask of a movement still battling barbarism in Mississippi. But we can agitate the right questions by probing at the contradictions which still stand in the way of the "Great Society." The questions having been asked, motion must begin in the larger society, for there is a limit to what Negroes can do alone.

THE MYTHS OF COALITION

Stokely Carmichael and Charles V. Hamilton

Stokely Carmichael, a former chairman of the Student Non-violent Coordinating Committee (SNCC), and Charles V. Hamilton, Professor of Government at Columbia University, reject a coalition with liberal-labor reform groups—with those who are economically secure. They argue for a coalition based on self-interest and oriented towards a limited, definable set of objectives, here seen in terms of a poor black-poor white alliance. As a form of ethnic politics, black political activists, independently organized, would present a list of demands for a black share in an affluent America.

What, then, are the grounds for viable coalitions?

Before one begins to talk coalition, one should establish clearly the premises on which that coalition will be based. All parties to the coalition must perceive a *mutually* beneficial goal based on the conception of *each* party of his *own* self-interest. One party must not blindly assume that what is good for one is automatically—without question—good for the other. Black people must first ask themselves what is good *for them*, and then they can determine if the "liberal" is willing to coalesce. They must recognize that institutions and political organizations have no consciences outside their own special interests.

Secondly, there is a clear need for genuine power bases before black people can enter into coalitions. Civil rights leaders who, in the past or at present, rely essentially on "national sentiment" to obtain passage of civil rights legislation reveal the fact that they are operating from a powerless base. They must appeal to the conscience, the good graces of the society; they are, as noted earlier, cast in a beggar's role, hoping to strike a responsive chord. It is very significant that the two oldest civil rights organizations, the National Association for the Advancement of Colored People and the Urban League, have constitutions which specifically prohibit partisan political activity. (The Congress of Racial Equality once did, but it changed that clause when it changed its orientation in favor of Black Power.) This is perfectly understandable in terms of the strategy and goals of the older organizations, the concept of the civil rights movement as a kind of liaison between the powerful white community and the dependent black community. The dependent status of the black community apparently was unimportant since, if the movement proved successful, that community was going to blend into the white society anyway. No pretense was made of organizing and developing institutions of community power within the black community. No attempt was made to create any base of organized political strength; such activity was even prohibited, in the cases mentioned above. All problems would be solved by forming coalitions with labor, churches, reform clubs, and especially liberal Democrats.

Subsequent chapters will present in detail case studies showing why such an approach is fallacious. It should, however, already be clear that the building of an independent force is necessary; that Black Power is necessary. If we do not learn from history, we are doomed to repeat it, and that is precisely the lesson of the Reconstruction era. Black people were allowed to register, to vote and to participate in politics, because it was to the advantage of powerful white "allies" to permit this. But at all times such advances flowed from white decisions. That era of black participation in politics was ended by another set of white decisions. There was no powerful independent political base in the southern black community to challenge the curtailment of political rights. At this point in the struggle, black people have no assurance—save a kind of idiot optimism and faith in a society whose history is one of racism—that if it became necessary, even the painfully limited gains thrown to the civil rights movement by the Congress would not be revoked as soon as a shift in political sentiments occurs. (A vivid example of this emerged in 1967 with Congressional moves to undercut and eviscerate the school desegregation provisions of the 1964 Civil Rights Act.) We must build that assurance and build it on solid ground.

We also recognize the potential for limited, short-term coalitions on relatively minor issues. But we must note that such approaches seldom come to terms with the roots of institutional racism. In fact, one might well argue that such coalitions on subordinate issues are, in the long run, harmful. They could lead whites and blacks into think-

ing either that their long-term interests do not conflict when in fact they do, or that such lesser issues are the only issues which can be solved. With these limitations in mind, and a spirit of caution, black people can approach possibilities of coalition for specific goals.

Viable coalitions therefore stem from four preconditions: (a) the recognition by the parties involved of their respective self-interests; (b) the mutual belief that each party stands to benefit in terms of that self-interest from allying with the other or others; (c) the acceptance of the fact that each party has its own independent base of power and does not depend for ultimate decision-making on a force outside itself; and (d) the realization that the coalition deals with specific and identifiable—as opposed to general and vague—goals.

The heart of the matter lies in this admonition from Machiavelli, writing in *The Prince:*

And here it should be noted that a prince ought never to make common cause with one more powerful than himself to injure another, unless necessity forces him to it . . . for if he wins you rest in his power, and princes must avoid as much as possible being under the will and pleasure of others.[1]

Machiavelli recognized that "necessity" might at times force the weaker to ally with the stronger. Our view is that those who advocate Black Power should work to minimize that necessity. It is crystal clear that such alliances can seldom, if ever, be meaningful to the weaker partner. They cannot offer the optimum conditions of a political *modus operandi.* Therefore, if and when such alliances are unavoidable, we must not be sanguine about the possibility of their leading to ultimate, substantial benefit for the weaker force.

Let black people organize themselves *first,* define their interests and goals, and then see what kinds of allies are available. Let any ghetto group contemplat-

[1] Niccolo Machiavelli, *The Prince and the Discourses,* New York: Random House (Modern Library), 1950, p. 84.

g coalition be so tightly organized, so rong, that—in the words of Saul Alin-y—it is an "indigestible body" which nnot be absorbed or swallowed up.[2] he advocates of Black Power are not pposed to coalitions per se. But we are ot interested in coalitions based on yths. To the extent to which black peo-e can form *viable* coalitions will the d results of those alliances be lasting d meaningful. There will be clearer derstanding of what is sought; there ill be greater impetus on all sides to liver, because there will be *mutual* re-ect of the power of the other to reward punish; there will be much less like-hood of leaders selling out their follow-s. Black Power therefore has no con-otation of "go it alone." Black Power mply says: enter coalitions only *after* u are able to "stand on your own." lack Power seeks to correct the ap-roach to dependency, to remove that ependency, and to establish a viable sychological, political and social base pon which the black community can unction to meet its needs. *B. p. note*

At the beginning of our discussion of lack Power, we said that black people ust redefine themselves, state new val-es and goals. The same holds true for hite people of good will; they too need redefine themselves and their role.

Some people see the advocates of lack Power as concerned with ridding e civil rights struggle of white people. his has been untrue from the begin-ing. There is a definite, much-needed le whites can play. This role can best examined on three different, yet in-rrelated, levels: educative, organiza-onal, supportive. Given the pervasive ature of racism in the society and the xtent to which attitudes of white supe-ority and black inferiority have become mbedded, it is very necessary that hite people begin to disabuse them-elves of such notions. Black people, as e stated earlier, will lead the challenge old values and norms, but whites who ecognize the need must also work in is sphere. Whites have access to groups

Saul Alinsky speaking at the 1967 Legal De-nse Fund Convocation in New York City, ay 18, 1967.*

in the society never reached by black people. They must get within those groups and help perform this essential educative function.

One of the most disturbing things about almost all white supporters has been that they are reluctant to go into their own communities—which is where the racism exists—and work to get rid of it. We are not now speaking of whites who have worked to get black people "accepted," on an individual basis, by the white society. Of these there have been many; their efforts are undoubtedly well-intended and individually helpful. But too often those efforts are geared to the same false premises as integra-tion; too often the society in which they seek acceptance of a few black people can afford to make the gesture. We are speaking, rather, of those whites who see the need for basic change and have hooked up with the black liberation movement because it seemed the most promising agent of such change. Yet they often admonish black people to be non-violent. They should preach non-violence in the white community. Where possible, they might also educate other white people to the need for Black Power. The range is great, with much depend-ing on the white person's own class background and environment.

On a broader scale, there is the very important function of working to reori-ent this society's attitudes and policies toward African and Asian countries. Across the country, smug white com-munities show a poverty of awareness, a poverty of humanity, indeed, a pov-erty of ability to act in a civilized man-ner toward non-Anglo human beings. The white middle-class suburbs need "freedom schools" as badly as the black communities. Anglo-conformity is a dead weight on their necks too. All this is an educative role crying to be performed by those whites so inclined.

The organizational role is next. It is hoped that eventually there will be a co-alition of poor blacks and poor whites. This is the only coalition which seems acceptable to us, and we see such a coali-tion as the major internal instrument of change in the American society. It is

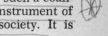
note

purely academic today to talk about bringing poor blacks and poor whites together, but the task of creating a poor-white power block dedicated to the goals of a free, open society—not one based on racism and subordination—must be attempted. The main responsibility for this task falls upon whites. Black and white *can* work together in the white community where possible; it is not possible, however, to go into a poor Southern town and talk about "integration," or even desegregation. Poor white people are becoming more hostile—not less—toward black people, partly because they see the nation's attention focused on black poverty and few, if any, people coming to them.

Only whites can mobilize and organize those communities along the lines necessary and possible for effective alliances with the black communities. This job cannot be left to the existing institutions and agencies, because those structures, for the most part, are reflections of institutional racism. If the job is to be done, there must be new forms created. Thus, the political modernization process must involve the white community as well as the black.

It is our position that black organizations should be black-led and essentially black-staffed, with policy being made by black people. White people can and do play very important supportive roles in those organizations. Where they come with specific skills and techniques, they will be evaluated in those terms. All too frequently, however, many young, middle-class, white Americans, like some sort of Pepsi generation, have wanted to "come alive" through the black community and black groups. They hav wanted to be where the action is—ar the action has been in those places. The have sought refuge among blacks from a sterile, meaningless, irrelevant life i middle-class America. They have bee unable to deal with the stifling, racis parochial, split-level mentality of thei parents, teachers, preachers and friend Many have come seeing "no differenc in color," they have come "color blind. But at this time and in this land, colo *is* a factor and we should not overloo or deny this. The black organization do not need this kind of idealism, whicl borders on paternalism. White peopl working in SNCC have understood this There are white lawyers who defenc black civil rights workers in court, anc white activists who support indigenous black movements across the country Their function is not to lead or to se policy or to attempt to define black peo ple to black people. Their role is sup portive.

Ultimately, the gains of our struggle will be meaningful only when consolidated by viable coalitions between blacks and whites who accept each other as co-equal partners and who identify their goals as politically and economically similar. At this stage, given the nature of the society, distinct roles must be played. The charge that this approach is "anti-white" remains as inaccurate as almost all the other public commentary on Black Power. There is nothing new about this; whenever black people have moved toward genuinely independent action, the society has distorted their intentions or damned their performance.

THE NEGRO IN POLITICS

James Q. Wilson

With the passage of the Civil Rights Acts of 1964 and 1965, the end of political power was fused with the end of political protest. The legal foundations of discrimination were destroyed, and the civil rights movement was faced with the job of eliminating other vestiges of inequality

*·y strategic innovation. Some of the objectives remaining were the fus-
·ng of political with direct action, the winning, replacing or rejecting of
·olitical allies, and the choice of remaining reformist or becoming trans-
ormed into a revolutionary body.*

*·n both the North and the South, there were problems of getting blacks
·egistered and encouraging them to vote, of overcoming apathy (and in
·he South, overt or covert intimidation), and of offering the potential
·lack voter a candidate and a program that was meaningful to him. In
·addition, there was the further problem of party affiliation. The argu-
·ment was made for bolstering the liberal forces within the Democratic
Party, especially important now that the movement's goals went beyond
the single question of civil rights. It was suggested that a coalition could
be made with the progressive elements within the country (trade unions,
liberals, religious organizations) and thus transform these blocs into an
effective political majority.*

*In examining the prospects for change through political action, James Q.
Wilson, Associate Professor of Government at Harvard University, out-
lines the problems attendant upon forming coalitions in both the South
and the North. In some areas of the South, a coalition of blacks with the
white, urban, upper middle class (the commercial and industrial elites)
may work—witness Atlanta; in other areas, however, there may be a
trend towards independent black politics, especially where blacks constitute a majority. In the North, paradoxically, conventional politics plays
a less relevant role for several reasons. First, traditional party loyalties
are strong and dependable enough to insure that blacks will remain
Democratic. Also, political issues are class rather than race centered, and
socio-economic welfare legislation is passed by coalitions of labor unions
and liberals which need not include blacks. At best, black politics in the
North is "marginalist politics."*

I. THE NEGRO VOTER IN THE SOUTH

A useful oversimplification is that, in the South, the enemy of the Negro is the lower- and lower-middle-class, particularly rural, white, and the ally of the Negro is the upper-middle-class, particularly urban, white. Since Reconstruction, the Bourbons and the Populists have engaged in intermittent political warfare; occasionally the Negro has been used—particularly in the last two decades of the nineteenth century—as an ally of one white class against the other, while at other times—particularly in the first half of the twentieth century—he has been disfranchised in order to prevent him from being allied with either class. The political suppression of the Negro did not, as C. Vann Woodward makes clear, occur immediately after the withdrawal of Union troops but only after the white community, divided along class lines, discovered that the competitive wooing of Negro votes created a politically unstable situation best resolved by eliminating the Negro vote —and thus the Republican party—and bringing the white majority into the dominant Democratic party.[1]

But the Negro is no longer disfranchised, except in Black Belt counties; probably one-third of the potential Negro vote has been registered, and more gains can be anticipated. Negroes of voting age constitute one-fifth of the adult

[1] C. Vann Woodward, *The Strange Career of Jim Crow* (New York, 1957), pp. 38–47, 60–68.

From *Daedalus*, XCIV (Fall 1965), 959–973. Reprinted with permission of *Daedalus*, Journal of the American Academy of Arts and Sciences, Boston, Massachusetts. *The Negro American*, The Daedalus Library, Houghton Mifflin Company, 1965.

population of the eleven Southern states but less than one-twelfth of the registered Southern voters. If another 570,000 Negroes can be added to registration rolls now estimated to contain nearly two million Negroes, half the potential Negro voters will be eligible. In those areas where the Negro vote is already significant, the politics of a "Second Reconstruction" seem to be emerging—with the important difference that the Negro may no longer be franchised if competition for his vote proves unsettling.

Negroes, when they vote, can cause a startling change in the style, if not the substance, of Southern politics. Segregationists will have to choose between abandoning race-baiting as a political tactic or getting out of politics. (The prospect of large numbers of politicians quitting politics—especially in the South, where politicians are shrewd and politics is a way of life—seems, to say the least, remote.) And politicians who are by nature inclined to entertain sympathetically legitimate Negro demands will be encouraged to entertain them publicly. For example, Rep. Charles L. Weltner, Democrat of Georgia, voted against the 1964 Civil Rights Act when it first came before the House in February, 1964. By July, however, when the bill came back from the conference committee for final passage, he had changed his mind and voted in favor of it. It does not detract from the moral quality of Weltner's bold action to note that between the two crucial votes the governor of Georgia signed into law a bill to redistrict the state's congressional seats in a manner that substantially increased the proportion of enfranchised Negroes and decreased the porportion of lower-middle-class whites in Weltner's district.[2]

In the past, at least, neither political party could take the Southern Negro vote for granted. A majority of their votes twice went to Dwight Eisenhower

and frequently were cast for Republica candidates in such cities as Atlanta an Louisville. In 1960, many—though no all—Southern Negro precincts voted fo President Kennedy; in 1964, almost a of them supported President Johnson.[3]

The independence—which, to the pol itician, can mean only uncertainty—o the Southern Negro vote has variou causes. One, of course, is that the South ern Democratic party has so conspicu ously been the enemy, its candidates i all but a few cases outbidding each othe in defending segregation. Another is tha the issue confronting the Southern Ne gro in many elections is clear and dra matic: which white candidate scores lowest on the segregation scale, this be ing, for the Negro, the only important scale. Unstable politics is here the result of single-issue politics. A third reason is that potential Negro political leaders, being largely excluded from an active role in both the majority party and the increasingly "lily-white" Republican minority party, have not been co-opted by the system. Negro politicians, without permanent organizational commitments to white leaders, have been free to deliver Negro votes to whichever candidate or party seemed most attractive in each election. Where the Negro leader was corrupt, he delivered the vote in exchange for tangible considerations,[4] where honest, in exchange for intangi-

---

[2] Rep. Weltner voted against final passage of HR 7152 on February 10, 1964. On February 17, the United States Supreme Court ordered redistricting in Georgia (Wesberry v. Sanders, 376 U.S. 1 [1964]). The Georgia Senate, anticipating the ruling, had already passed a redistricting bill on February 12; the House followed suit on February 21. The governor

signed the bill into law on March 10; it divided Weltner's old district into two new districts—Weltner's (the Fifth), consisting of Fulton County (Atlanta); the other (the Fourth) consisting of suburban DeKalb County. As a result of this change, the percentage of Weltner's district which was Negro rose from 26.5 to 33.3. Weltner voted for House acceptance of the Senate-amended Civil Rights Act in July. An interesting analysis of Weltner's relationship to the Negro vote is M. Kent Jennings and L. Harmon Zeigler, "A Moderate's Victory in a Southern Congressional District," *Public Opinion Quarterly*, Vol. 28 (Winter 1964), pp. 595–603.

[3] In 1968, they went for Humphrey. [Editor's note.]

[4] Alfred B. Clubok, John M. Degrove, and Charles D. Farris, "The Manipulated Negro Vote; Some Pre-Conditions and Consequences," *Journal of Politics*, Vol. 26 (February 1964), pp. 112–129. This is not confined to the South. In 1964, certain Negro precincts in Harrisburg, Pennsylvania, voted for Senator Goldwater while Northern Negroes elsewhere were voting ten-to-one for President Johnson. One can only speculate on the ways by which that extraordinary result was achieved.

le concessions.[5] Negro politics in the South has yet to be professionalized, and hus the distinction—commonplace in he North—between the (usually moderate) party hierarchy and the (often militant) civic and "race" leadership has not become widespread.

To say that the Southern Negro political leadership is unprofessional does not mean that it is either unskillful or unsuccessful. In those cities or counties where the Negro voter is neither terrorized nor apathetic, he is capable of voting with almost incredible unanimity and precision, at least for the most visible offices. When Ivan Allen, Jr., ran against Lester Maddox in 1961 for mayor of Atlanta, Negro precinct 7-D gave Allen 2,003 votes, or 99.9 per cent of the total, and Maddox 4 votes. Since there were five white voters living in the precinct, it is quite likely that Allen got *all* of the Negro votes—an almost unbelievable feat of organization and communication, especially when one recalls that Allen was a wealthy white businessman who was scarcely an all-out integrationist.[6] The single-issue politics of the South has produced a form of political behavior among Negroes and whites which is highly rationalistic and extraordinarily sophisticated.[7] Voters become exceptionally sensitive to almost imperceptible differences in the positions candidates take, publicly or privately, on "The Issue" and go to considerable lengths to conceal group preferences lest premature revelation prove counterproductive.

In the South, more than anywhere else, a deliberate balance of power politics may be practiced in which viable coalitions may be formed. The most important and most successful example of this is what might be called the Atlanta Coalition. Formed in the 1950's by Mayor (now "Mayor Emeritus") William B. Hartsfield and continued by Mayor Ivan Allen, Jr., it is, stripped to its essentials, a tacit alliance between upper-middle-class whites and Negroes against lower-middle-class whites. In even blunter terms, the Bourbons and the Negroes have voted together to exclude the rednecks from power in the city. There are, of course, strains in the alliance. The more militant Negroes are restless with the leadership of the Atlanta Negro Voters' League and with what they regard as the insufficient progress in race relations under Hartsfield and Allen. White businessmen, in turn, often feel the mayor has gone too far, as when Allen testified before Congress in favor of the elimination of segregation in public accommodations. Furthermore, it is not clear that every Southern city could put together such a coalition even if it wanted to do so. Come cities have lost their Bourbons to the suburbs (Atlanta carefully annexes all upper-income suburbs and avoids annexing any working-class suburbs) while others have a business leadership that is composed of small shopkeepers rather than a commercial and industrial élite concerned with establishing the city as a great regional center.[8] And in some cities, such as New Orleans, the Negroes themselves have been unable to create a stable and effective political organization representative of all elements of the community.[9]

Whatever the limitations or difficul-

---

[5] Cf. H. Douglas Price, *The Negro and Southern Politics: A Chapter of Florida History* (New York, 1957); Bradbury Seasholes and Frederic N. Cleaveland, "Negro Political Participation in Two Piedmont Crescent Cities," in F. Stuart Chapin and Shirley F. Weiss (eds.), *Urban Growth Dynamics* (New York, 1962), pp. 265–270; Henry Holloway, "The Negro and the Vote: The Case of Texas," *Journal of Politics*, Vol. 23 (August 1961), pp. 526–556. These Negro voters' leagues are effective only if they operate within the consensual framework of the Negro community. Price (on page 72) notes that a "league endorsement of a wrong candidate in a contest where a clear difference in attitude toward the Negro exists does not swing many Negro votes; rather it raises the question, 'who sold out?' " Holloway (on pages 539–540) observes that "Negro leaders don't have the power to deliver a bloc vote at will. . . . The Negro voter has his own fairly constant voting propensities which leaders disregard at risk to themselves."

[6] Jack Walker, "Negro Voting in Atlanta: 1953–1961," *Phylon*, Vol. 24 (Winter 1963), pp. 379–387.

[7] Negro voting in many Southern cities is an empirical case of the rationality model suggested in Anthony Downs, *An Economic Theory of Democracy* (New York, 1957).

[8] The Atlanta Coalition is described in Edward C. Banfield, "Atlanta: Strange Bedfellows," in *Big City Politics* (New York, forthcoming).

[9] Daniel C. Thompson, *The Negro Leadership Class* (Englewood Cliffs, N.J., 1963), pp. 112–114.

ties, however, there can be little doubt that the natural ally of the Southern Negro, for the foreseeable future, is the cosmopolitan white bourgeoisie.[10] In part, this reflects self-interest: race conflict is bad for business, destructive of property, and productive of unfavorable national publicity. In part, it reflects an enlarged conception of the common interest: Negroes have a moral right to vote, to be free from arbitrary arrest, and to be protected from official abuse, even if century-old prejudices require that the Negro not live next door to whites. The issues now being pressed by the Negro in the South make the most fundamental claims of elementary justice; when the claims of simple justice are reinforced by self-interest, the potential for effective action is great. But this white ally has little interest in a massive redistribution of income, the nationalization of political authority, or the reordering of society.

In the Black Belt, where Negroes outnumber whites, such alliances are hard to create. In Mississippi, there seem to be no allies whatsoever. It is precisely in such areas that a more radical Negro politics is emerging, though it is still so apocalyptic in its vision and unrealistic in its methods that it can point to little progress. The Freedom Democratic party won a great victory at the Democratic National Convention in Atlantic City, but the radical leadership which now appears to influence it not only rejected that convention's seating compromise but seems intent on rejecting all compromises with what, to it, is an essentially corrupt and hypocritical society.[11]

Given the massive, unyielding, and violent nature of white resistance to Negro demands in many Black Belt counties, it is not hard to understand some of the attitudes of the increasingly radical Negro political leadership. Early and measured accommodation to Negro political demands has, in many Southern cities, led to the emergence of relatively moderate Negro leaders and of a Negro strategy emphasizing limited objectives. But the Black Belt has not, except in a few cases, made concessions—in part because Negroes there are in the majority and in part because such largely rural or small-town areas lack a white upper class of sufficient size and strength to challenge white extremists.

There are some Black Belt counties where Negroes can and do vote, but ironically the gains that have accrued to them from politics in these areas are less than the gains from politics in areas where Negroes are a minority but where social and economic conditions are more favorable to political organization, articulation of demands, and bargaining over changes in the welfare or status of Negroes. Where Negro voting has occurred in the Black Belt, it has meant (in general) the cessation of police abuse and administrative discrimination, the appointment of Negroes to certain government positions, and higher expenditures on public facilities in Negro neighborhoods.[12] It has rarely meant general integration of schools or public accommodations or new public works programs to improve Negro living conditions. The financial resources and community tolerance for such efforts simply do not exist. White voters do not even approve such projects for themselves. By contrast, in some of the highly urbanized areas where Negroes vote but are in a distinct minority, a combination of factors—the availability of tax resources, a well-organized white political structure with which bargains can be struck, and a large and self-sufficient Negro leadership class—makes it easier to translate votes into substantive gains.

All this suggests that the substantive,

[10] Survey data on the importance of education (and class position) for the racial attitudes of Southern whites can be found in Herbert B. Hyman and Paul B. Sheatsley, "Attitudes Toward Desegregation," *Scientific American* (July 1964), pp. 16–23, and Melvin M. Tumin, *Desegregation* (Princeton, N.J., 1958). But Matthews and Prothro, using ecological correlations, show that the level of education among Southern whites must be very high before it affects Negro voter registration rates. Donald R. Matthews and James W. Prothro, "Social and Economic Factors and Negro Voter Registration in the South," *American Political Science Review*, Vol. 57 (March 1963), pp. 36–38.

[11] The situation changed to one of compromises in the 1968 convention and the trend seen there will probably continue to grow, giving rise to growing black influence in the Southern Democratic Party. [Editor's note.]

[12] United States Commission on Civil Rights, *1961 Report* (Book 1, Part 3).

rather than psychological, consequences of Negro voting in Black Belt counties are not likely to be so great as the diehard white resistance might imply. The resistance itself, however, should it continue for long, may change this significantly. When the social, economic, and political demands of a group are linked with a protracted and bitter struggle for the franchise, the members of that group are more likely to acquire a permanent sense of political identity and a more intense commitment to the goals of the group than would be the case if substantive goals were asserted long after the frenchise had been won. (One of the reasons—there are many—that no socialist or labor party developed among American workers may be that their major economic demands were made long after the franchise had been acquired without a struggle.)[13] The campaign for the vote now developing among Southern Negroes is likely to have profound effects on subsequent Negro political organization and tactics, for the campaign can generate morale, a sense of unity (the vote is a wholly instrumental objective that permits otherwise competing leaders to submerge their differences), and an independence from traditional party loyalties.

Discussion, in such states as Mississippi, of the possibility of a Negro political party suggests one alternative—in my judgment, a disastrous one—to the pattern of coalition politics now being practiced outside the Black Belt. For the Negro vote to be (potentially) the marginal vote, it is not enough that it be an uncommitted vote. Since Negroes in every Southern state are a minority (although in some states a very large one), it is also necessary that the white vote be divided. . . .

Dividing the white vote will not be easy under the best of circumstances, but it is not likely to be easier if Negro political strategists either elect to form a separate party or emphasize objectives which draw closer the white cosmopolitan élite and white lower-middle-class extremists. Continued Negro pressure,

with federal assistance, for the franchise and for the observance of constitutional and legislative guarantees will utimately divide the opposition; broadening Negrò demands at this time to include more radical objectives may unite it. This may be an expression of the willingness on the part of the bourgeoisie to support demands for *liberty* (the franchise, legal justice, and equal access to public facilities) but to oppose demands for *equality* (the elimination of intergroup differences in income, occupation, and place of residence). Negro-white coalitions in the South, where they exist at all, are by and large libertarian rather than egalitarian in purpose. . . .

Coalition politics is important not only because of the need for allies, but also because of the problem of motivating Negro voters. As a result of their low socio-economic position, getting Negroes to register and vote even after all administrative barriers have collapsed can be very difficult. . . . Surprisingly high voter participation can be obtained, however, when the contest is important *and the Negro vote may decide the outcome.* In the Allen-Maddox election in Atlanta, for example, 80 per cent of the registered voters in nine predominantly Negro precincts turned out to vote; by comparison, only 69 per cent of the registered voters in ten predominantly lower-income white precincts voted.[14] (Negroes participate less than whites in elections for offices less visible than mayor; they also register in slightly smaller proportions.) Although there is no direct evidence on this, it seems likely that the remarkably high Negro voter turnout in cities like Atlanta might be much lower if the candidate supported by Negroes had no chance of winning— as would be the case if he did not have the backing of a substantial block of white voters.

II. THE NEGRO VOTER IN THE NORTH

It is in the North that politics as conventionally practiced seems less relevant to the needs of the Negro. This may appear paradoxical, given the great importance attached to the Northern urban

---

[13] Seymour Martin Lipset, *Political Man* (Garden City, N.Y., 1960), pp. 84–85.

[14] Walker, *op. cit.*, p. 384.

Negro vote in influencing contests for President, governor, and senator.[15] It is of course true that the Negro is concentrated in areas of high strategic significance for state-wide or national political candidates. The Negro vote for President Kennedy was, in several Northern industrial states, greater than the margin by which Kennedy carried those states. The same, however, can be said for the Jewish vote, the Catholic vote, and the labor vote. With so many apparently marginal votes cast, a President might be forgiven if he allowed himself to be paralyzed by the competing demands of their spokesmen. . . . In Congress, the Negro vote is likely to have a much greater long-run effect in the South than in the North. Over *half* of all Southern congressional districts in 1963 had a population that was one-fifth or more Negro. In the North and West, by contrast, fewer than one-twelfth of the districts had so high a proportion of Negroes.

Furthermore, the civil rights legislation so far enacted has been directed primarily at remedying discrimination against the Negro in the South—in voting, public accommodations, and the like. To the extent that Negro political influence in the North contributed to the passage of these bills, it was influence wielded on behalf of Southern Negroes and as part of a much larger liberal coalition in which religious organizations played an exceptionally important role.[16] Further legislative progress on behalf of Southern Negroes is still possible; the question, however, is what progress can be made on behalf of Northern Negroes and what political tactics should be used.

The utility of politics to the Northern Negro is limited for a variety of reasons. First, his traditional party loyalties are strong and thus his vote, particularly in general elections, is less likely to be uncertain. There are some obvious exceptions to this pattern, of course. In cities such as Boston, where party organization is almost nonexistent and where an attractive Negro candidate can be found in the Republican party, Negroes will cross party lines in very large numbers. (Edward Brooke, the Negro Republican Attorney General of Massachusetts, carried Negro precincts by margins of ten to one at the same time that Democrat Lyndon Johnson was carrying these precincts by margins of fifty to one.) In most of the largest Northern cities, however, the only question surrounding the Negro vote in partisan elections is its size rather than its direction.

Second, the major issues confronting the mass of Northern Negroes are economic and cultural rather than political or legal. Rustin is entirely correct in saying that "at issue, after all, is not *civil rights*, strictly speaking, but social and economic conditions."[17] The paradox is two-fold. On the one hand, American political institutions provide no way for the organized political pressure of a particular disadvantaged group to reshape in any fundamental sense social and economic conditions. Whereas the identity and political obligations of a sheriff or a governor can profoundly affect the lives of Negroes in the South by determining whether or how they will be intimidated or harassed, the election of a public official in the North rarely has any direct or obvious consequences for the average Negro voter. (It is *because* it makes so little difference, of course, that Northern party leaders have found it relatively easy to instill traditional party commitments in Negroes. A simple decision rule—such as "vote Democratic"—is more economical, for both the party and the voter, than the kind of elaborate and subtle group interest calculations that occur where, as in the South, the outcome *is* important.)

That is not to say that it makes no difference which party or faction controls the White House or Congress. The prob-

[15] The 1964 and 1968 presidential elections bear this out. [Editor's note.]
[16] The importance of political factors other than the Negro vote in obtaining civil rights legislation is illustrated by the state adoption of "open occupancy" laws barring discrimination in the private housing market. The first states to pass such laws were typically states with a very small Negro population. See James Q. Wilson, "The Negro in American Politics" in John P. Davis (ed.), *American Negro Reference Book* (New York, forthcoming).
[17] *Commentary* (February 1965), p. 26.

bility of there being certain kinds of redistributionist and welfare programs enacted does depend on election outcomes, but not in a way that makes it possible for any particular voting bloc to hold any particular public official responsible for such programs. Such considerations ought to be borne in mind when one evaluates assertions about the "alienation" of the urban voter, particularly the low-income Negro. That politics seems irrelevant to their daily preoccupations is not necessarily an expression of neurotic withdrawal or separateness but may well be the rational conclusion of a reasonably well-informed citizen.

The other paradoxical element is that, when major programs *are* launched to deal with basic social and economic conditions, they are likely to be the product of a political coalition in which the persons whose lives are to be changed play a relatively small role. The recent federal programs to deal with delinquency, poverty, and housing were assembled by bureaucrats, professors, and White House politicians. The most dramatic of these—the "war on poverty"—did not come about, as Daniel Patrick Moynihan makes clear, as the result of any great upsurge of popular demand.[18] Nor were these programs aimed explicitly at the "Negro problem." Indeed, it might have been much harder to get them adopted if they had been defined as "Negro programs." (In fact, some of these programs—particularly the antipoverty program—were in part intended by many of their supporters, probably including the President, to dampen the civil rights "revolution" by improving the material condition of Negroes.) At the local level, public expenditures for the benefit of the poor are often authorized in local referenda elections in which the civic leadership as well as a substantial portion of the votes come from upper-class whites who join with lower-class Negroes to secure the adoption of measures which, if they were national rather than local matters,

these whites would oppose.[19] Rich suburbanites will favor free medical care for the indigent if the issue is stated in terms of building a new county hospital and is voted on locally but not if the issue is called "socialized medicine" and is voted on in Washington.

All this suggests that the Negro is in need not of a single grand alliance, but of many different and often conflicting alliances which take into account the different bases of support available for different kinds of issues. Nationally, organized labor may support civil rights and income-transfer measures but locally it is often likely to support (at least tacitly) segregated housing and economy in government. Religious groups are very effective when the issue is voting rights; they are much less effective in dealing with economic questions where simple morality is not at issue. Upper-class businessmen may support Negro voting claims in Southern cities and Negro oriented public works programs in Northern cities, but nationally they will oppose large-scale income redistribution. A grand Negro-liberal coalition, if achieved, may so rationalize these inconsistent positions as to deliver the leadership of would-be allies into the hands of those elements who are least in favor of (or least effective on behalf of) Negro causes. Nowhere are these problems better seen than in the relationship between Negro and white workers in our major industrial cities.

While it may be true that Negroes and whites have a common interest in ending unemployment, improving housing and education, and resisting technological displacement, a stable and enduring alliance to attain these objectives will not be easily achieved. The only major political mechanism by which poor whites and Negroes have in the past been brought into alliance—the big-city machine—is collapsing; except for a few large industrial unions, no substitute has yet appeared.

Only Philadelphia and Chicago, of the

[18] Daniel Patrick Moynihan, "Three Problems," an address given before the Conference on Poverty in America at the University of California at Berkeley, February 26–28, 1965 (mimeo).

[19] James Q. Wilson and Edward C. Banfield, "Public-Regardingness as a Value Premise in Voting," *American Political Science Review*, Vol. 58 (December 1964), pp. 876–887.

larger Northern cities, have strong city-wide machines (that is, political parties based on the distribution of material rewards). In these areas, Negro and white political leaders are paid to work together, albeit for very limited objectives; Negro and white voters, in turn, are induced by door-to-door persuasion to vote together, particularly in primaries.[20] Such organizations cannot endure much longer, for the resources at their command are diminishing. When they collapse, Negro political leadership will fall into the hands of men who can find effective substitutes for organization: personal charisma and bellicose militancy (such as that of Adam Clayton Powell in New York or Cecil Moore in Philadelphia), expertise in factional manipulation and strategic alliances (such as that of J. Raymond Jones in New York), or successful appeals to middle-class white voters and white political leaders (such as that of Edward Brooke in Massachusetts or Augustus Hawkins in Los Angeles).[21] Yet to emerge, but certain to come, are Negro political leaders who will obtain their major support from the more militant civil rights organizations. In only a very few cases does there seem to be much likelihood of organized political coalition between white and Negro workers similar to that found from time to time in Detroit. The United Auto Workers, and to a lesser extent the United Steel Workers, have, through the political action of integrated locals, elected carefully balanced tickets of Negro and white politicians.

Even under UAW leadership, the Negro-white workers' coalition has been subject to tensions. The most important of these has been the necessity of emphasizing economic objectives that do not require social reorganization (such as integrated housing) close to home. The UAW cannot deliver votes of white workers for liberal mayors or those of Negro workers for conservative mayors

without great difficulty. Furthermore the coalition was created in a period c rising demand for workers; how it wi function when Negroes and whites ar competing for a decreasing number c jobs remains to be seen. (The fact tha the locals are integrated and that a elaborate code of seniority rules has bee devised may help reduce what might oth erwise be a starkly racial conflict ove jobs.) Finally, no one should allow him self the comfort of believing that Pres dent Johnson's massive victory ove Barry Goldwater disproves the existenc of strong anti-Negro sentiments amon many white Northern Democratic voters At most it suggests that, faced with complex political decision involving is sues of foreign relations, economic pol icy, and welfare programs as well a civil rights, the white worker decide that peace and security were, under th circumstances, more important than reg istering a protest against Negro claims.

The area in which this latent conflic between Negro claims and white resist ance is most likely to erupt is that o public safety and administration o criminal justice. It is one of the few is sues (schools are another) in the Nortl over which a clear political contest car be waged. The police are highly sensitiv to the explicit and implicit directives of local elective officials; unlike economie issues, a political victory here can have direct and immediate—although per haps not drastic—consequences for Ne groes. The white concern over "violence in the streets" and unchecked criminalit is not (as critics of Goldwater charged) simply a rhetorical mask for opposition to civil rights demonstrations or even for anti-Negro sentiment (though it involves a significant element of this). Polls taken by both parties during the campaign suggest that Johnson was never able to meet this issue effectively; perhaps a majority of voters thought Goldwater was best able to handle this problem.[22] For the Negroes, the issue of "police brutality" and police corruption is probably the single most effective appeal

[20] James Q. Wilson, Negro Politics (New York, 1960), Chs. ii, iii, iv; and James Reichley, The Art of Government: Reform and Organization Politics in Philadelphia (New York, 1959).
[21] Edward C. Banfield and James Q. Wilson, City Politics (Cambridge, Mass., 1963), chap. xx, discusses alternative Negro political styles.

[22] See Election '64, a report of the Ripon Society (Cambridge, Mass., 1965), p. 29.

or the mobilization of mass Negro protest activity, particularly among rank-and-file lower-income Negroes. Many middle-class Negroes will, of course, admit privately that they, too, would like to see the police check criminal behavior among lower-class Negroes, but it is becoming increasingly difficult for them to say this publicly.[23]

What is remarkable is that so few candidates for mayor or governor are openly exploiting white fears of crime, particularly Negro crime.[24] In part this is because too many of them must face Negro voters who would immediately interpret such views as anti-Negro prejudice even if, in fact, prejudice had nothing to do with it. And in part this is because there is a deep and general distrust of the police among upper-middle-class whites, particularly white liberals, such that it is often better politics to be "anti-cop" than "anti-Negro." On this issue, even more than on the issue of income redistribution, the natural Northern ally of the Negro is the white liberal.

It is, of course, fashionable today to attack the "white liberal" as hypocritical on civil rights issues. After all, he is likely to live in a "lily-white" suburb, attend a "lily-white" church, and perhaps teach in a university with no Negroes on its faculty. And the white liberal, in the eyes of Negro radicals, makes the fatal error of believing that meaningful change can be accomplished within the present political, social, and economic system. By accepting the system, he accepts the necessity of compromise, and compromise is seen as both morally wrong and practically unworkable.

All this misses the point, which is that the white liberal is, in the North, one of the Negro's *only* significant allies in a situation in which allies are essential. He is not and cannot be an all-purpose ally, however. The upper-class business or professional man is a more useful ally in the South where, by halting and

nervous steps, his support is being mobilized to achieve voting rights and end police abuse; he is also a more useful ally in the North when the issue is legitimating a local public welfare program. The principal value of the white liberal, on the other hand, is to supply the votes and the polical pressures (increasingly mobilized through religious organizations) that make it almost suicidal for an important Northern politician openly to court anti-Negro sentiment.

The alliance, however, is as much tacit as explicit. If Negroes increasingly distrust liberals (because they are both ideologically suspect and rivals for power), liberals have had difficulty finding Negroes who have both a genuine mass following and a commitment to what the liberals regard as appropriate means and ends. The hoped-for alliance in Manhattan between liberal Democratic reform clubs and Harlem political leaders has not materialized to any degree.[25] The most popular Negro leader in Philadelphia, Cecil Moore, is regarded with incredulous disdain by white liberals. Negro machine politicians, such as William Dawson of Chicago, are rejected by both those middle-class Negroes and those middle-class whites whose commitment to social change exceeds their faith in the Democratic party leadership.[26] Negroes, such as Edward Brooke, whom white liberals find attractive are usually prevented by their position (that is, being responsive to a largely white constituency) from being in the visible forefront of civil rights campaigns. The cause of most of this unrequited love is that the Negro has come of age politically at a time when not only machines are collapsing, but

[25] James Q. Wilson, *The Amateur Democrat* (Chicago, 1962), Ch. ix, discusses reform-Negro relations.
[26] In Chicago, certain white and Negro civil rights groups ran a Negro candidate (A. A. Rayner, Jr.) against Rep. William L. Dawson in the 1962 Democratic primary. Dawson won, easily carrying the lower-income Negro precincts but losing (by as much as two-to-one) many middle-class Negro precincts. The Dawson organization is very strong among lower-income Negroes, particularly those in public housing projects.

[23] In this connection, cf. Northern appeal of George Wallace in the 1968 presidential election. [Editor's note.]
[24] The 1969 mayorality races in some large cities like Los Angeles, Detroit, New York give little cause for optimism on this score. [Editor's note.]

the whole lower-class style of politics—the politics of friendships, trades, patronage, and neighborhood localism—is falling into disrepute. Negroes are expected to climb a political ladder which, as a result of several decades of successful reform efforts, is now missing most of its rungs. For whites, vaulting to the top is easy—television is one way; converting an established business or civic reputation into appointive and elective office is another. But the Negro community lacks the business and civic infrastructure which is necessary to convert private success into public office. Enough money has yet to be earned by enough Negroes to produce a significant precipitate of Negro civic statesmen.

Negroes know this and therefore are demanding that economic differences between Negroes and whites be eliminated. If the white liberal reformer is to be allowed to abolish the system by which political and economic progress was once made, then he must (many Negroes argue) replace it with something better. The Negro demand for economic equality is no longer, as Nathan Glazer points out, simply a demand for equal opportunity; it is a demand for equality of economic *results*.[27] American politics has for long been accustomed to dealing with ethnic demands for recognition, power, and opportunity; it has never had to face a serious demand for equal economic shares. Thus, in the North as well as the South the principal race issue may become a conflict between liberty and equality. This may be the issue which will distinguish the white liberal from the white radical: the former will work for liberty and equal opportunity, the latter for equal shares. This distinction adds yet another complication to the uneasy liberal-Negro alliance.

If the alliance is hard to sustain today, it will be subject to even greater strains in the future. The Northern Negro community, lacking a single clear objective and a well-organized and unified leadership, will continue to be volatile. Protest demonstrations will reveal less discipline than those in the South and the likelihood of violence will be greater. The church simply does not have the importance to the Northern Negro that it does to the Southern, nor are the targets in the North so visible as those in the South. The Negro riots of the summers of 1964 and 1965[28] in Harlem, Rochester, Chicago, Brooklyn, Los Angeles, and elsewhere were not in any obvious sense "race" riots (that is, riots of Negroes against whites in protest against claimed injustices) or the outgrowth of civil rights demonstrations. But whatever their cause (simple hooliganism was an important element) their lesson for genuine civil rights demonstrations is clear: there is always a potential for violence, particularly when the demonstration is as much against indifference as against injustice.

That the movement is badly organized, understaffed, and threatened by violence does not mean it is ineffective. As other sources of power decline in strength, the power of the civil rights organizations increases. It is not yet possible for them to *elect* candidates, even in all-Negro districts, to many significant offices, but it is entirely possible for them to *prevent* someone else from being elected, even in heavily white districts. In most Northern cities, there are now a small number of Negro civil rights leaders whose reputation is such that their concerted opposition to a Negro candidate would prevent his election. They are often strong enough to hurt the chances of white candidates by casting on them (rightly or wrongly) an "anti-civil-rights" label which will be the kiss of death for white liberal (and even not-so-liberal) voters. As one Negro leader in Boston, a hopelessly unorganized city, told me recently, "We are entering a new political era of guerrilla warfare in which the lack of organization and discipline will not be nearly so important as the possibility of well-placed sniping at the enemy."

[27] Nathan Glazer, "Negroes and Jews: The New Challenge to Pluralism," *Commentary* (December 1964), p. 34.

[28] And, one might add, those of 1966, 1967, and 1968 as well. [Editor's note.]

Competition to get the pro-civil-rights label (or, more accurately, to avoid getting the anti-civil-rights label) will become more intense. The 1964 presidential campaign may well have facilitated this process by involving Negroes in unprecedented numbers both as voters and as campaigners. The intense opposition to Goldwater resulted in Negroes registering as Democrats in overwhelming proportions in both North and South. The Democratic National Committee mobilized ministers, barbers, beauticians, and other strategically placed Negroes as volunteer campaigners. Nationally known civil rights leaders, particularly Martin Luther King, toured the country giving ostensibly "nonpartisan" speeches, urging Negroes to vote but not telling them whom to vote for (that was hardly necessary). Only time will tell what effect Goldwater will have on Negro political loyalties (particuarly in the South, where they have been in doubt) and on the number and style of Negro political activists. It is possible, though far from certain, that 1964 will have fixed Negro political loyalties in the same way that Al Smith in 1928 and Franklin D. Roosevelt in 1936 fixed white loyalties and will bring into politics a new cadre of Negro leaders just as 1952 and 1956 brought in new white cadres. Regardless of whom the Republicans nominate, the Democrats will be running against Goldwater for the next twenty years.

Apart from building fires under politicians, there remains the question of what Negro (or Negro-white liberal) politics can accomplish. Simply electing more Negroes to public office will make some difference, for politics depends as much as anything on communication. Groups not in a position to know in time cannot act in time; protest as a strategy is better suited to *blocking* change than to initiating it, and this requires a good intelligence network. . . . Furthermore, the greater and more direct involvement of the federal government in the affairs of cities and metropolitan areas under circumstances which require that federal authorities not visibly deny the pre-

cept of equal justice for all means that Negroes, through injunctive procedures as well as political pressure, will be able to compel changes in the administration of local programs in schools, housing, and the like as a precondition to receiving the growing volume of federal aid.[29]

In those areas where elective officials administer and are directly responsible for programs affecting the lives of Negroes, Negro voting strength will, of course, be important. One such area is the administration of justice. In the South, the impact of Negro enfranchisement on these practices could be revolutionary; even in the North, Negro political power can significantly constrain mayors and police chiefs. (The mayor of Detroit, Jerome Cavanaugh, attracted widespread—and possibly decisive—Negro electoral support because of Negro discontent with Detroit police practices under the previous administration; immediately upon assuming office, Cavanaugh replaced the police commissioner and supported efforts to alter police behavior in Negro neighborhoods.) Education is another area where elected officials can sometimes be held accountable to the voters. But here the Negro voter faces a paradox: in cities (such as New York) where Negroes are sufficiently numerous to be taken seriously by politicians, they are also so numerous as to make a solution to the problems of racial imbalance or low standards in the public schools very hard to find. Where (as in Boston) Negroes are sufficiently few in number to make solutions possible (at least in principle), they are also so few as to be a relatively inconsequential political force.

Negroes, in short, will increasingly be able to play marginalist politics. But this approach rarely produces wholesale or fundamental changes in the life chances of large numbers of people. Some Negro (and white) leaders, recognizing the limitations of conventional politics, are suggesting new forms of organization. One of these is the power-oriented neigh-

[29] Title VI of the Civil Rights Act of 1964 will facilitate challenges.

borhood association, exemplified by The Woodlawn Organization (TWO) in Chicago.[30] Such groups mobilize Negroes (or lower-income voters generally) by defining and dramatizing adverse local conditions which are the result of the indifference or hostility of outside forces, such as the city administration or nonresident white businessmen. Relying on indigenous leadership, the organization mounts a neighborhood protest against the outside "enemies"; by blocking proposed changes or by effectively challenging current programs, the group acquires the power to bargain with outsiders, especially city politicians and administrators. Demands are made and enforced concerning the appropriate kinds and levels of city services to be provided in the area.

The key to this strategy is the effort to build an indigenous political organization which is not part of the city-wide political apparatus and thus is not subject to its constraints. The paln is to fill the vacuum created by the decay of the ward organization of city-wide machines by substituting a nonpartisan but power-oriented civic association which seeks to provide collective rather than divisible benefits (such as patronage) for its members and followers. Since it trades in general rather than individual benefits, the civic association must find new ways to motivate its members; it does so by relying on a combative ideology. There are at least two major problems with this strategy, however. First, the resources with which to sustain such an organization are very scarce. It obviously cannot rely on government or business support (although the recent history of New York's Mobilization for Youth, patterned in many ways on the TWO model, suggests that at least in the immediate future it may be possible to use government funds—such as federal antipoverty or antidelinquency money—to launch organizations aimed at challenging government policies). Foundation and philanthropic support is available (TWO was begun in this way),

but such support depends on the pr grams of the action groups being co sistent with what middle-class whit liberals who operate foundations will to erate. In short, it depends on a Negr liberal white alliance.

The second problem is that it ma prove difficult to generalize such a stra egy. Building a coalition of sever neighborhood combat organizations n cessitates finding the terms on whic groups with essentially local interest can work together. This is difficult eve for a traditional political party whic can control patronage and nomination for office. A nonpartisan neighborhoo association, on the other hand, whic attempts to maximize benefits for it area often must do so at the expense o other areas; this potentially competitiv situation may make collaboration diff cult. A coalition might, of course, b formed out of a common allegiance to candidate for major political office, bu this means accepting the constraint (principally, moderation) that inevita bly accompany electoral contest.

III. THE NEGRO VOTER IN THE FUTUR

In short, the possibility for an effec tive radical Negro political strateg seems remote and the effort to achiev it costly. In the South, the potentia supporters of at least current Negro ob jectives are the members of the com mercial and industrial élite. Althoug they are everywhere slow to emerge and in some places wholly absent, there is a present no reasonable alternative. At lanta is an example of both the strengths and weaknesses of such an alliance even there, of course, it rests on a deli cate population equilibrium which could be upset should either the Negroes be come too numerous or the upper-class whites too few. What will happen after federal intervention has opened the bal lot box to Negroes in the Black Belt counties remains to be seen. There are very few precedents from which one might infer predictions about political behavior when Negroes are in the majority in a city or county and vote. (In Washington, D.C., Negroes are the voting majority, but there are few issues

[30] Charles Silberman, *The Crisis in Black and White* (New York, 1964), Ch. x, describes TWO.

' substance to decide.) There are some
outhern communities which are over
) per cent Negro and in which many
though not all) Negroes vote. Little is
nown about them except that, while
the franchise has ended harassment by
ublic officials and law enforcement of-
cers, it has not revolutionized the living
onditions of the Negroes. Perhaps the
afest prediction is that the vote will
ave very different effects in different
laces. In some communities, patron-
ge-based Negro political machines will
merge; in others, non-ideological Ne-
ro-white alliances will develop; in still
thers, militant and even radical Negro
movements will appear (particularly,
erhaps, in parts of Mississippi where
the young cadres of SNCC and the
reedom Democratic party have begun
) instill a radical ideology, though not
et to build a serious organization). In
eneral, the type of Negro political or-
anization which emerges will depend
rucially on the type of white political
rganization already in existence.

In the North, the Negro, facing goals
nore complex and less clearly moral
nan those faced in the South, will con-
nue to require white liberal, business,
nd union support for slow progress to-
vard programs productive of income,
ducation, and wider opportunities. The
rban vote already greatly influences the
residential election; how much more it
vill influence state and congressional
lections now that reapportionment is
pon us is uncertain. It will clearly be
n state legislatures that the Supreme
Court's edict will fall most heavily. Con-
ress is not likely to be revolutionized;
ndeed, there is some evidence that an
bsolutely equal apportionment system
night *strengthen* the "conservative"
ote.[31] In any case, the role of Congress
s more the product of our localistic
olitical structure than of the appor-
ionment system, and this is not likely
o change significantly for a very long
ime.

Negro-labor alliances will still be pos-
ible, but like all such alliances in
American politics they will be *ad hoc*,
imperfectly organized, and difficult to
sustain. From the point of view of the
Negro, one of the chief advantages of
the American political system is surely
that the "undemocratic" convention and
caucus system by which political parties
are governed makes possible *leadership*
coalitions that, while not based on a per-
fect fusion of interests and aims, are
not without influence in the choice of
candidates and even the outcome of elections. Indeed, to the extent political parties are made internally more "democratic"—by abolishing conventions in
favor of primaries, by reforming the
governance of local political organizations, and by flooding the deliberations
of party leaders with the merciless light
of publicity—these coalitions may become more difficult to assemble and sustain, for an informed rank and file requires leaders who emphasize rather
than compromise the very great differences which now separate, for example,
white and Negro working-class voters.

The fact that many different alliances
must be maintained will not only call for
a high degree of tactical flexibility; it
will probably also mean that the civil
rights movement will remain divided and
even at war with itself. The divisions
among Negro leaders are the result not
simply of personal rivalry or organized
ideology, but of the effort to adapt a
movement to the necessity of simultaneously occupying incompatible positions
in order to draw strength from others.

The various white partners in these
alliances will themselves be changed by
civil rights activity. The nonpolitical
strategies developed by the Negro for
gaining bargaining power—the sit-in,
the protest march, and passive resistance—have already been adopted by
whites concerned with everything from
American foreign policy to university administration.[32] Physically obstructing the
operation of an organization—often ille-

* Andrew Hacker, *Congressional Districting*
Washington, D.C., 1963), pp. 87–91.

[32] Recently, internes protesting the pay policies
of a California country hospital practiced a
"heal-in." They flooded the hospital with pa-
tients, many not in need of hospitalization, in
order to overload the organization and thus
acquire bargaining power vis-à-vis the administration.

gally—has, in the 1960's, become a commonplace method for attempting to change the behavior of that organization. This "spill-over" of civil rights tactics into other areas of social conflict has probably been one of the most important consequences of increased Negro militancy.

Because of the structure of American politics as well as the nature of the Ne-

gro community, Negro politics will ac complish only limited objectives. Thi does not mean that Negroes will be con tent with those accomplishments or re signed to that political style. If Negroe do not make radical gains, radical sen timents may grow. How these sentiment will find expression is perhaps the mos perplexing and troubling question of all

AN INTERRACIAL MOVEMENT OF THE POOR

Carl Wittman and Thomas Hayden

At the time of the writing of their article, Carl Wittman was a student and president of the Swarthmore Political Action Committee. Thomas Hayden was a graduate student at the University of Michigan. Both had worked closely with the Students for a Democratic Society.

Opposed to coalition politics, they advance here the case for independent political action. Rather than allying with the Democratic Party, perceived as a structural component of neo-imperialism, the warfare state and short-range reforms, the authors emphasize the need for working with the poor, the students and other alienated groups in order to form a radical movement in opposition to the existing power structure. To coalesce with liberals, they argue, was to compromise with radicals; to work within the existing social order and be assimilated into the present American society, was to forego the chance to create a new social order and a new value structure.

In their concern with alliances, Wittman and Hayden analyze the prospects for a coalition between blacks and whites, especially between the poor sub-groups of each race.

As desegregation proceeds, what are the possibilities for alienation between the Negroes and their real or possible white allies? The areas of possible alienation are twofold: between Negroes and *all* whites, and between Negroes and *poor* whites.

In the first instance, there is a kind of black nationalism that works uneasily within the integration movement itself. In many organizations there are disputes and splits over the color of leadership: whether whites understand Ne-

groes or Negroes understand whites whether whites, particularly whit women, can be effective as organizer in the Negro community. These issue are among the most sensitive and diffi cult we face, and undoubtedly they wil continue for an indefinite period of time We suspect, however, that the tension in the movement will not be resolved or the side of an official black nationalis ideology, partly because it has not hap pened yet between Negroes and white in general even in the worst condition

Reprinted from *The New Student Left: An Anthology* (Beacon Press, 1967), pp. 182–192, 194 211, edited by Mitchell Cohen and Dennis Hale.

of racist tyranny. Even were it to develop in some organized form, we would guess that at some future time the possibility of Negro-white alliances would reappear because a program based primarily on race will not improve the terrible social conditions which provide the impetus for the movement. A permanent alienation should not develop unless two groups continually interfere with the deepest economic interests of each for a sustained period of time. . . . As long as the Southern Negro does not directly threaten the white's livelihood by actually taking his job or destroying the quality of the white child's education (and hence livelihood in this society), such estrangements are not permanent and can end whenever whites clearly see it is in their economic interest to unite with the Negro.

One clear example of this happened in Cambridge, Maryland: six months of intensive race warfare over the issue of a public accommodations referendum, with poor whites providing the core of segregationist action and opinion. Only a month later, however, the United Packinghouse Workers organized three locals in Cambridge, on a racially integrated basis, with militant Negro leadership carefully avoiding anything which would upset the 40 per cent white membership. After one of the locals was recognized, the victory party included dancing, drinking, and eating in racially mixed company, previously taboo in the town, and it occurred without incident. Without the movement, the Cambridge power structure could have defeated the union drive as it did in the past. The built-up alienation on the part of the poor whites was subordinated to a common interest which happened to be central to the lives of black and white factory workers.

Of course, we are aware that estrangement between the races can continue indefinitely, as it has in the South for a century. We are haunted not only by Southern history but by the problems dividing Muslims and Hindus in India, and Negroes and East Indians in British Guiana. But we remain convinced so far that permanent alienation can be avoided and overcome by a serious movement which fights for the interests of both groups. We know of almost no effort to organize in white communities in the South—and it would be foolish to be either optimistic or pessimistic until actual experiments are further underway. We need to know much more about the organizing problems faced by the Negro-white-Mexican coalition in Texas, and whether those problems are applicable to other areas of the South; we need to know much more about rank-and-file feelings within the white working class; we need to make contact with whatever radical individuals there are within the Southern union bureaucracy. These needs are briefly mentioned here to suggest some gaps in our present knowledge; the implications for our proposed or actual organizing campaigns remain to be discussed in a later section of these comments.

We realize that much of the preceding can be applied directly to the Northern civil rights situation, and that this is a symptom of the nationalization of the problem and the movement. Since the North is the place we generally work, however, there is need for a more detailed picture of trends.

Observed from the angle of current social alignments, the movement in the North seems pointed directly towards a difficult and violent period. As a movement it has developed very rapidly, with the mass base of support emanating from the metropolitan ghettos that run all across the northern rim of the country. There seem to be distinctive Northern conditions which tend to make the protest movement immediately volatile in relation to the white community. These are: first, the official but betrayed policies of non-discrimination; second, the change of the North into a "treadmill" instead of a "ladder," due to the automation of traditional low skill work; third, the greater isolation of the ghetto-dwelling Negro from the world of white people. These seem to be conditions conducive to militant tactics, distrust of promise, and a concern for radical economic improvement.

Various integrationist and separatist movements are now developing, most of them threatening the real or apparent interests of many whites, who now are so actively opposing the pace of integration that they can loosely be called "counter-revolutionary." Between these two contending forces, there is a crisis and a paralysis among the liberal organizations, and behind it all is the Federal Government encouraging mild concessions and preparing to maintain order. When looked at this way, it seems that a stalemate is likely to continue temporarily and then turn into a polarized and violent disorder ending in government intervention—without a change in the grim conditions of poverty and exploitation which are their irritants. We could speculate endlessly in this direction, but at a point it becomes fruitless because there is no way to predict reliably what will happen in the next few months.

There is another way to approach the problem which is more manageable because it avoids the problems of such sweeping prediction. This is through classifying various demands which are being made by the movement, and judging, first, the extent to which they might solve problems if they were enacted, and, second, the effect of these demands on existing or potential alliances with white groups.

The demands seem to fall into four categories:

1. *Demands to eliminate discrimination or de facto segregation.* These traditional and worthwile demands would rectify a discriminatory situation, and the rectification would materially improve the Negro community. The prominent issues are open housing, fair hiring practices, and the end of gerrymandered school and voting districts. The major forces behind these demands in the Negro community are persons of middle-class aspirations, who may or may not be militant, for these barriers alone prevent their entrance into the mainstream of American life. Lower-class Negroes support these demands with conviction also, but more out of a belief that a basic change would occur if the demands were met. This seems to be supported by much evidence that the lower-class Negro prefers *improved* schools over *integrated* schools, and generally *improved* living conditions over *integrated* living conditions.

These demands have the full support of the liberal white community, for legal equality and equality of opportunity are part of the liberal ideology. No doubt the ire of the white unemployed, or working class, or voting property holder is sometimes heightened by many of these insistent Negro demands, but there is hardly any infringement of basic interests here.

2. *Demands which symbolically assert Negro dignity but neither achieve change nor alienate whites very much.* Examples of these are the anti-blackface demonstrations in Philadelphia, and demands for Cleveland school integration (integrated schools in poor white areas continue to segregate students by classroom).

These issues are pushed often by militant leaders who appeal to the racial bitterness of the Negro community for effective mobilization on further issues, or in some cases, unfortunately, for power without regard to the needs of the Negro community. These demands also receive lower-class Negro support because of the channel which they provide for the vigorous expression of a justifiable anger—but as with the first class of demands, these are not directed towards very much change in the economic conditions of segregated life.

However, the possibility of enraging or alienating liberal, middle- or lower-class whites with these demands is much greater than with the first set. The kind and depth of alienation is very important to consider here. It is not a case of *direct* economic deprivation being forced on the white, and in that sense it does not create what we tend to think of as permanent alienation. However, the impact on some whites is almost this severe, especially in the case of school integration. The experiences in Cleveland, where a lower-class Italian mob intimidated a CORE demonstration out of their neighborhood (over a question which clearly should be resolved on the side of the Negroes), and in New York where thousands of middle-, lower-middle-, and lower-class parents, without much visible coordination, gathered to protest the "pairing" of schools, demonstrate the immediate significance of this question. What is behind this "counter-revolutionary" response? All of the parents are in some sense racist, and this is one of the few occasions forcing a public declaration of their feelings—this is part of it. But the very fact that the racism was not so manifest before this might indicate that it is a feeling of secondary importance to the white person. What seems to bring it into prominence is the feeling that the proposed integration will destroy the "quality" of the school and prevent their youngsters from getting the education necessary to fit into the highly-skilled professions, those being the few left today which are at all secure. Is this a realistic fear? If it is, then this issue might create permanent alienation because, next to personal livelihood, the destruction of a son or daughter's future is perhaps the most serious threat which can be made to a parent. But on the other hand, if the fear of the white parent is not realistic, then the alienation probably can be overcome. We are inclined to think that the fears are very unrealistic. American education is responsive often to local parents' pressures, and "forced" integration probably will be coupled with the improvement of educational conditions for both black and white children. In addition, it is unlikely that there will be very extensive joint racial attendance at schools of the poorest ghetto groups and the white upper-middle classes because of their geographical and jurisdictional separation. As for the integration of lower- and lower-middle class groups, the threat of integration is likely to lead to either 1) the evacuation of the white groups from the area, if they are financially able, or 2) the actual integration of the whole neighborhood, with the resulting great potential for seeing common problems. In either case, there is not a serious long-term threat of severe alienation of the white community no matter how militantly the Negro movement presses the issue. Our tentative conclusion is that despite the initial antagonisms of the confrontation, there is relatively little danger of permanent alienation. But there is little direct social change either, since the fundamental need is for *more* and *better* education. The positive gains lie in the stir and pressure for change created in the various white communities, and the greater militancy and grass roots community focus of the Negro movement.

3. *Demands which are specifically racial, do not achieve very much, and potentially alienate large numbers of whites.* The clearest and most prominent example of this kind of demand is that of replacing white workers with black ones in a situation of chronic unemployment. Sometimes there is inarticulate anger behind this kind of demand, and sometimes there is a complicated theory of change. Usually the theory is that a violent clash over scarce employment opportunities liberates the Negro from self-doubt, makes alliances possible, and forces the middle and upper classes to act decisively to improve the economic and racial situation of the country.

Other issues of this kind are less clearcut. The demand for a white student to lower his immediate educational chances by being bussed to a deprived Negro school might fall in this category instead of the second one, as we suggested before. So might the moving of a Negro into an economically insecure white neighborhood, although a violent white lower-class status reaction in these circumstances is not likely to be permanently alienating. Even the demand for fair employment sometimes might create alienating consequences, especially when it is seen as whites giving up jobs to fulfill Negro desires, or splitting the pie evenly. In small cities like Chester, Pennsylvania, where communications are relatively good between various groups, the idea that a job given to a Negro is a job taken from a white is quite obvious and unacceptable to all. In a larger city, however, this humanism is missing, perhaps because of the anonymity of the metropolis; in addition, the rude fact that there just are not enough jobs for everyone is much more difficult to see. Thus, the tendency to push harder and more vigorously for fair employment in the great industrial centers might be perceived as a by-product of racial encroachment more than as a failure of the national economy. Where unemployment is not so chronic as to convince everyone of its central importance in their problems, and yet severe enough to make one race threaten the other, tensions might be highest. At a certain point, the question of whether unemployment should be a "fair" situation for everyone could become less important than the question of how everyone can fight together for full employment. In many Northern cities we now face this delicate and potentially creative balance of feelings. (A part of this issue is what relation the Negro movement and the labor movement will have. Under increasing pressure from Negroes, the labor movement might decide to face squarely the problems of automation and stagnation, or they might see themselves as part of the privileged industrial elite fighting down the challengers.)

As we approach the end of legal discrimination in this country, we can expect the movement to debate—often with bitterness—the value in making this kind of demand for *racial* economic change as opposed to the demand for *class* economic change. The race-centered demand, which is the more alienating of the two, can find broad Negro support today although the new middle-class leadership will be pushing it the hardest. We should note the occasional unwillingness of the lower-class Negro, at least in Cambridge and Chester, to make demands that the white lose his job or that a white child lose his education, even when proposed by the militant leadership. These reflect some of the class differences *within* the Negro movement.

It is quite unreasonable, however, to expect that the Negro movement always will want to avoid alienating demands. Those who believe in the potential of an interracial movement, however, should be concerned with the dangers in this kind of demand and consider arguing against it, perhaps even at the risk of losing their voice in the Negro movement.

4. *Demands for political and economic changes of substantial benefit to the Negro and white poor.* Examples of these include improved housing, lower rents, better schools, full employment, extention of welfare and social security assistance. They are not "Negro issues" *per se;* rather, they are precisely those issues which should appeal to lower-class whites as well as to Negroes. They are difficult demands around which to organize, most probably for two reasons. The first is that they may lack a racial content and therefore might not be easy to shift towards in a movement with a heavy racial emphasis. But this can be overcome, for example, if these demands are linked with racial ones—if the issues of full employment and non-discrimination in hiring are linked. The second, and much more serious, reason is that no such demands can be realized on the community level. New York, for instance, is thoroughly unable to find even the resources needed to improve housing conditions in Harlem even if the city wants to; similarly, Chicago cannot conceivably use its available resources to fully retrain the Negro unemployed—and each of these problems is only a fraction of the entire condition of poverty that needs to be attacked in a nationally planned, financed, and integrated way. This in absolutely no way negates the importance of raising issues locally which can be solved only by national social change. But it suggests that in the absence of national social change, which is impossible to expect in the shortrun, these demands in themselves may not result in the small victories which are required, presumably, if a movement is to keep its spirit. It suggests further that in the near future there might be a need for an organized national agency representative of the common interests of these local protest groups and able to mobilize and focus pressure that can be felt at national levels.

These difficulties are compounded by a leadership problem. The support for

hese demands comes most of all from
ower-class Negroes and political radi-
als of all classes, races, and occupa-
ions. Much of the time the injection of
hese demands into the existing move-
nent will be opposed by the middle-class
eadership which prefers the first three
inds of demands. Such leaders are
ikely to have everything to gain and
nothing to lose by the introduction of
uch issues.

Some mainstream organizations will
hy away from this approach on the
grounds that conservative support for
ivil rights will be lost if the issue is
oined with proposals for broad new gov-
rnment economic policies. This is to be
xpected and, although differences need
not be inflamed, they should be recognized as real since such new policies *are*
needed. At any rate, nearly all the lib-
ral institutions will go along in rhetoric
vith such demands, but few will follow
up with a massive action program to
nake rhetoric reality. The Negro move-
nent, where it believes in these demands, is usually more committed to a
nass movement than are the sympa-
hetic but lethargic white-led organiza-
ions. This failure of the liberal Left to
:ome through with a total commitment
o all the discomfort of a political cru-
sade is another cause of the present lack
of support for these demands in the Negro movement. Why should the Negroes,
crushed as they are with a very specific
'orm of exploitation, be called on to
:reate a general social program and then
vait for the whites to organize? Part of
our whole crisis so far is that the white
person has nothing specific to point towards when the Negro asks for *proof*
:hat an interracial movement is possible. This is partly the reason for the importance of our present work in Chi-
:ago and Appalachia which involves
white unemployed people. But it is important to remember that even if lower-
:lass whites suddenly materialized as a
mass movement looking for Negro allies
in the struggle for dignity, there would
be—and there are even when the question is raised today—immense difficulties rooted in the possible threat to certain Negro leaders. One SNCC member
from Mississippi, in a recent Atlanta
meeting, suggested that the "dream"
of a Southern neo-populist movement
would be a direct threat to the Negro
organization to the extent that the organization is a means of finding and expressing a Negro identity.

Before taking up these questions of
interracial relations, the prior question
is: What do we know or believe about
the possibilities of organizing with the
other ethnic minorities and the white
poor? Any discussion of a movement of
the poor is incomplete and utopian without such an appraisal.

THE POSSIBLE ALLIES OF THE NEGRO MOVEMENT

Economic deprivation is not an experience peculiar to the Negro in America.
It is a class experience which cannot be
overcome by a single race. Thus any
potential allies of an economically oriented Negro movement will be the class
affected by this phenomenon. The essential class unity of a group must not
be overlooked: Any united movement
must stress this, the only common
ground which all members of the group
share. Their common consciousness of
poverty and economic superfluousness
will ultimately have to bring them together.

However, at this stage, when only the
Negroes are conscious of the possibility
for real change, and when no more than
rumblings are heard elsewhere, a general call to the depressed groups in society is not likely to have much success.
The problem of deprivation is felt differ-
ently by countless groups, the major dividing characteristics being *ethnic identity, age, place,* and *occupational status.*

Ethnic Groups

Apart from the Negro, the other distinct ethnic groups are the Spanish-
speaking Puerto Ricans and Mexicans,
and the communities of southern and
eastern Europeans in the large cities.

*   *   *

All these ethnic groups share with the
Negroes a key position in American so-

ciety: They are segregated, separated, and exploited. For as long as they have been in the "land of opportunity," this has been the case. The other generations of migrants, organized labor, and the midwestern farmers were all dealt into the more protected lower-echelons of the establishment in the twenties, thirties and forties. The crisis today rests largely on the fact that the orthodox manner of dealing people in, even if all white Americans ceased their racism, is disappearing as automatiion cuts into the mass production centers of the economy. The very segregation of the colored ethnic groups, however, has led to problems concerning the prospect for alliances. Differences, often divisive ones, exist between the Negroes, Puerto Ricans, Mexicans, and Indians. But it seems possible to bridge many of the differences which impede a political alliance, especially as the peril of slump and the promise of a movement become more sharply counterposed. But whether ethnic-centered demands will be accompanied by demands for general economic change does not depend solely on the existence of a long-term slump or the spontaneous development of a new consciousness. It depends also on organizing experiments which we have not begun.

Of groups in the urban North which might be directly antagonistic to the Negro movement, we must mention the eastern and southern Europeans, who are in the anxious lower sector of the establishment. A number recently immigrated here, especially after the 1945–48 transformation of eastern Europe, but the vast majority stem from the immigration waves of the late nineteenth and early twentieth centuries. They were the manual labor of the early industrial revolution in America, and were part of the industrial union movement. As a consequence, today they are mostly manual laborers in highly paid industrial sectors. They form a large part of the group of Americans who are lower class in status but middle-class in income.

Often they remain in the center of the industrial cities, however, and now are often contiguous to the expanding Negro ghettoes. They should not be seen primarily as a constituent of the American poor, but rather as a group which finds itself defending its position. They are threatened by automation, which is striking hard at the jobs the old ethnic minorities possess. But they are threatened also by the Negro movement in a number of ways. Their children are more likely than the Negro children to win the few jobs which will be remaining in the production sector of the economy—the artisan, craft, service, and new technical fields. This is due, of course, to their being white and having some money. But the point is that the Negro demand for decent jobs threatens many of these groups directly. In addition, the "encroachment" of the Negro on the border of their territory is threatening. They struggled for a long time to arrive where they are, and the increasing proximity of the Negro threatens their new-bourgeois position. Still further, although their schools are not much better in quality than Negro schools, education remains their key to the highly-paid jobs, and is seen with great protectiveness. . . .

These groups remain tightly-knit cultural centers, and have not been integrated completely into American society. They have been the centers of machine politics and the underworld. They have a well-developed system of mutual assistance and defense, and the violence of their response to the attack on their community's integrity may simply be a function of their need for this security. The breakdown of the neighborhood is especially a threat to them.

The conclusion we draw is that this group will play a reactionary role in the impending economic crisis. Unless they are hard hit by automation and can be organized around their employment status, it is difficult to see how outright conflict can be averted. The possibility of organizing them as ethnic groups around ethnic issues (such as the establishment of cultural centers) seems of no relevance to a coalition of forces demanding economic improvement. . . .

Age Groups

Age is another major factor in a discussion of potential members of our coalition, because America is organized to discomfort both its young and its old.

Some groups were either left out of, or arrived too late to partake in, the great establishment formed at the height of America's economic strength, and today they are undercut further by automation. This is precisely the case with the youth of America: They "arrived" in the labor force too late to fit in.

Among the hardest hit in the whole society is the young Negro. The insurgence of a demand for equality combined with his increased economic superfluousness in the South leads to rapid migration North. This rate reached 50 per cent for Mississippi Negroes in the 15–24 age group in the 1950–60 decade. Thus the youth's chances of getting work in the depressed center-cities of the North is even less than if he were older.

But, disregarding the race factor, the rate of unemployment for all high school dropouts and those who do not continue their education beyond high school is more than double the national figure. They are entering a labor force without skills necessary for a high paying job, but lack of education is not the major problem. Although it is true that any one youth can increase his chances for getting a job by acquiring a needed skill, the total number of unemployed will not decrease significantly if the level of education is raised.

The choice for the non-college youth is difficult: He must either break into the limited market for skilled labor, take a low-paying, insecure job in the service field, or fit into some niche that is open to him. The need for skilled labor remains, of course; traditional artisans (chefs, jewelers) are not threatened by automation, and the normal openings remain, through family contacts; the crafts (carpentry, plumbing, printing) absorb a small group. Those who are lucky can acquire the skills necessary for our new automated society (the electronics specialists, machine operators).

For the most part, however, especially in groups with any initial disadvantage (race, lower income, residence in depressed areas) the chances are that they will not get a secure, high-paying job. The four-dollars-an-hour industrial jobs which their fathers have are disappearing rapidly, industry by industry. Even in the most successful union settlements in automation-threatened industries, the best the union can get is a guarantee not to fire anyone; the ILWU contract on the West Coast last year is an example of a progressive union which realized that on a local or even industry-wide basis, this was the best they could do. Other unions, such as the United Mine Workers, have agreed to permit automation to proceed more rapidly, worrying only about those who maintain their jobs. In either case, the opportunities for youths entering the labor market are cut off completely.

Unless there is some niche (a job with a family firm, the opportunity to start a new business), chances are the youth will end up in a low-paying service job. Sales clerks, office-boys, managers of small retail stores and public accommodations are all unorganized, and wages rarely are more than the minimum required by law. Aside from the fact that $1.25 an hour is not enough to support a family in urban life, the crisis becomes more acute because of the standard of living which these youths are used to enjoying. Factory workers can afford to raise a medium-sized family in a middle-class area, but their sons will not be able to.

Thus a large group of what Labor Secretary Wirtz calls "out laws," the unemployed, or highly insecure youths facing a closing and formidable labor market, is growing constantly. These are perhaps the most invisible of the invisible poor, however—especially those who do not have some other identifiable characteristic (race, residence in a depressed area, etc.). It may be that the government is taking steps to avert a crisis before the group becomes politically vocal, or because of the correlation between crime and unemployed youth. The government program plans for the development of skills and mere labor-intensive work (CCC-type camps). To the extent that there is frictional unemployment, the skills program may reduce unemployment, although the ability of the government to carry on such programs successfully is at present seriously in doubt, judging from the slight success of the Manpower Redevelopment Program. The camps will reduce youth unemployment slightly, but it is not a permanent solution to the problem and may in fact heighten young people's consciousness of their common problems, the social and economic origin of such problems (as opposed to seeing it as individual failure), and the magnitude of the problems. . . .

Outside the Negro movement, there is a great deal of concern with the youth by educators, law enforcement officials, and social workers. Each interprets the problems of this group in his own light: The educators see the solution in a wider curriculum to help the student fit the new contours of the labor market; the law enforcement official will solve their problems by strict discipline and keeping them in school; and social workers see them as a product of poverty and broken homes, to be helped through careful understanding. But there has been no attempt to help this group see its own major problem—its uselessness in an automated society.

One of the priorities in research is to develop methods in working with these youth. They are particularly prone to right-wing and racist appeals, but perhaps must be organized around their own economic insecurities, and only observe later that their own demands coincide with those of Negroes. But broaching the race issues is not the only barrier which must be faced and overcome. The primary problem is finding them. Where this group overlaps with some other poverty category, e.g. race or depressed region, they are among the most vocal. But elsewhere it is likely that their frustrations will not be vocalized. In those cases where their parents are industrial workers making good union wages (and many of them will be from this group, for they most frequently

cannot find employment where their parents do), there is no reason why they will not subsist off their families until they reach an age when they think employment is easy to find. This does not mean that they are not potentially active, but only that, left alone, they will rarely give spontaneous verbalization to their real problems. It means that we must find concentrations of these youth, and after probing into their attitudes toward economics, employment, and race we must find a program which will appeal to them if possible, and fit into our concern for full employment. It seems likely that without a pressing sense of obligation (of the kind that a father who is laid off feels) and a group consciousness, they will not respond immediately to a call for direct action on economic issues. Alternative approaches which seem feasible are to begin organization on a smaller unit around those issues they deem important (social activities, police) or to tie them into another movement, presumably of white unemployed who have already entered the labor movement. . . .

Organizations by Area

Although the problems of the economy are nationwide, the poverty which results is not spread evenly to every nook and cranny of the country.

The depressed areas include:

1. Appalachia, including the southern tier of New York state, all of Pennsylvania, West Virginia, eastern Kentucky, and Tennessee, western Maryland, Virginia and North Carolina, and northern Alabama. This area suffers from the automation of the coal industry, the depressed railroads, and the general economic malaise. Northern Minnesota and Michigan's Upper Peninsula share this area's depressed mining conditions.

2. The industrial metropolises, including practically every major city in the north: Washington, D.C., Baltimore, Philadelphia, Boston, Pittsburgh, Newark, etc.; the string of small cities from Wilmington, Delaware, to Newark, New Jersey; the north-central areas of Buffalo, Cleveland, Akron, Cincinnati, Dayton, Detroit, and Chicago, and much of the West Coast.

3. The depressed agrarian areas: the Black Belt, stretching from eastern Louisiana across much of Mississippi and Alabama, through central Georgia, most of South Carolina, and south-central Virginia; the eastern shore of Maryland; southern Delaware, southern New Jersey, and northern New England.

4. Isolated cities and regions which are hit by cancellation of federal contracts, changes in world prices, and other unexpected crises; presently Long Island and upstate New York are representative.

The territorial basis of organization should be carefully considered. Not only are economic conditions varying on the regional, state, and municipal level, but political organization may be appropriate on these levels and on the ward and neighborhood levels as well. It is clear that solutions to the problems of these areas are only at the national level, however, and it continually must be kept in mind that such organization is strictly a means to exert pressure nationally and to gain strength for the movement, and not an end in itself. . . .

The major problem with organization on this level is that while it contains the most opportunity for new values, it is not the locus of decision-making. Only a block clean-up, anti-rat campaign, and at most a rent strike can be organized here with any material changes possible. . . .

Outside the industrial areas, a regional approach seems more viable. The Black Belt has been the target of voter registration, and the shared problems of Appalachia make it optimum for regional organization.

In translating local insurgency around economic issues into political terms, the same question of location is relevant. On the precinct ward level, the most one can do is publicize issues, and perhaps shake up the machine by destroying traditional patronage channels and even winning a city council election in one or more constituencies. Even on a city-wide level, only limited solutions to problems exist. . . . Direct political action can probably only force others to make concessions in their benefit, and not actually displace the rulers. On the other hand, the destruction of reactionary machines may well lead to urban renewal and some material benefit (although the tax base of those places where poverty exists is usually lower than in richer communities). In addition, the popular frustration created in seeing the inability of the municipality to act to solve basic problems brings on a greater consciousness of scope and depth of those problems. The election to state and federal legislatures of representatives who are liberal, and at least will not block reform, is a worthy bi-product of the movement, especially when it does not destroy the race and class identity of the people.

On the state level, there is a great possibility of effecting reforms through direct and political action. Again, however, those states which contain the largest incidence of poverty are least able to afford such programs as quality education, adequate welfare, and area redevelopment. Little except publicity and some reform can come on this level. . . .

Ultimately, however, the national level is where political pressures must be directed. This pressure undoubtedly will take many forms: Mass demonstrations, independent and reform Democratic candidates, and other activity might well be coordinated by a nationally-representative assembly of the movement. This is a very intricate problem, especially since the Negro movement is at this stage already, while its national liberal-labor allies live in impotent desperation below the establishment. How and whether to work out a national political organization is a problem which will require much sensitive exploration in the days ahead.

Organization by Occupation and Employment Status

The concept of organization by occupation and employment status is basic to this discussion, and is the last major criterion. Our premise is that a movement can be developed among persons whose economic role in the society is marginal or insecure. What groups, then, fall into this category by this criterion?

First, the *unemployed* present an important potential force. Due to the high levels of unemployment among Negroes, the civil rights movement is growing more militant in its demands and program. It is not at this point a chronic problem for whites, as mentioned earlier —a situation which leads to many of the tensions within the disadvantaged class. However, there are many instances of white unemployment; areas where highly skilled men are being laid off because of military shifts is just one example. And unemployment very definitely is a chronic *threat,* if not yet a reality, to whites. . . .

. . . There is good reason to question whether objective conditions (the social psychology of the unemployed, and the pace of unemployment itself) permit effective organization. Some unemployed whites may be more embarrassed than Negroes by their unemployed status, and see their problems as personal or obscure rather than social and clear. Many are not working because the only jobs they can get are not lucrative enough to compete with welfare or the other means of obtaining income. Some are too disillusioned by past disappointments. Others are just momentarily unemployed, the rapid turnover and transient nature of this group being one of its characteristics. These feelings are all supported by the fact that the problem is not always chronic and because few institutions express a real concern about it. In addition, many of the unemployed will be hard to find, since they are not registered and receiving unemployment compensation checks.

However, these qualifications by no means apply everywhere, and two growing forces could reduce much of their significance. The first is the expanding rate of unemployment which could become a chronic problem for whites unless drastically new ameliorative policies are enacted. The second is the growing visibility of the unemployment problem and the consequent incentive to see it as an issue on which action legitimately can be taken. Together these trends are likely to create a far greater consciousness and movement by the unemployed themselves. The better unions as well are likely to become involved in the political organization of their unemployed or the unemployed generally. In this case, organizing work might become easier for us, although new problems of remaining fraternal but independent in relation to the unions would arise. . . .

An even larger group defined by their job status is the mass of *employed but economically-insecure* persons—heralded in traditional ideology as the true agency of social change, but today a perplexing and divided group.

These often are reactionary people many trying to consolidate the achievements made during the generations since their families immigrated here. Many in the craft unions, which are organized to defend a single skill in a tightening market situation, are very likely to be racist and conservative. A good example is the building trades unions who, in New York, fought bitterly to preserve their racism and nepotism against the Negro jobs movement. It is likely that such persuasion will have to come in the streets as well as at the negotiating tables.

The industrial unions seem more likely to sense the need for progressive economic change, but today they might be tied too deeply to the Democratic Party and private enterprise to be a mass political force campaigning for a transformation to planning and abundance. So long as this is the case, the possibility for alliances between labor's rank-and-file and Negroes or the whole underdog class is jeopardized. Often the unions are fighting for the jobs of those who are working already, and the best they can hope to achieve on an industry-wide scale in the face of automation is an agreement that the machines will proceed no faster than the pace of natural turnover through retirement or quitting. Thus the union local, or any other local institution, cannot do very much by itself; it is modeled to work on a local level around local issues, and the problems it is confronting here are national ones that stretch beyond even their industry. Therefore, even though the rank-and-file is capable of more militancy than the union leadership much of the time (as the rising numbers of contract rejections, wildcat strikes, and various attitude surveys indicate), this potential militancy may be blocked indefinitely, rather than drawn out and channeled into political action.

We will be in a sensitive situation in this area, because our immediate identification is with the Negro movement and the problems of the unorganized poor—and these are not the primary and immediate constituents of the American labor movement. We should take up several opportunities for organizing work with the employed union men, however. One need is to attempt building political coalitions in places such as those on the West Coast—but coalitions spurred by the intensity of the Negro movement, not coalitions which compromise the Negro movement for the sake of its less militant allies. Another need is to engage directly in support of strikes where locals request assistance and where we can be of aid, make close contact with the rank-and-filers, and learn the techniques of strike organization. A third need is to participate in union educational programming; it seems possible, for instance, to help develop curricula on social problems to be used in many of the summer and year-round labor institutes and forums. A last need is to be involved directly in the labor movement with others of our persuasion, making an informal "legitimate" radical force pushing for policy and leadership changes and supporting and pressing the most militant wing of the CIO leadership.

Another potential participant in our coalition is the migrant worker, often described as the worst off and the most exploited of society's poor. Students and some unionists have attempted either labor organization or educational improvement among these poor, never with a great deal of success. Some of the problem seems to be the failure of the AFL-CIO to commit itself seriously enough in the southern California drive, but the problem of organizing in this area runs deeper than the matter of commitment. It may be the case that if the migrant worker were to "win" on the issue of unionization or wage-hikes, the growers would introduce the automatic machinery which they have been holding back while labor exploitation was so cheap. In that case, which we think is probable, the future for the migrant is coming to resemble that of the rural tenant or field hand being replaced by machines. Although there is no sign of a slowing of migration, ultimately the migrants may recognize the lack of opportunity in the cities and will remain where they are, unemployed, or join the welfare rolls in the North as the next best alternative. If they stay south, organizing becomes a separate problem; if they come north, they dissolve into the groups we are discussing.

In summary, there are various open possibilities for organizing among the 50 million or more "non-Negroes" who now are in a state of poverty or economic insecurity. What we know does not point towards anti-Negro or fascist attitudes throughout these groups of the poor, contrary to what some premature defeatists declare. We find a diverse series of situations, but most of them are characterized by:

1. The impact of growing economic insecurity.

2. A widespread feeling of alienation and a discouragement with existing economic policies.

Now with an official "war on poverty," there is a chance that the poor will feel a greater common consciousness of the legitimacy of their problems and the inadequacy of government programs. In addition, it is striking to observe that almost no attempts are being made to organize the poor for social change—and no verdict can be reached until a long-term attempt is made.

INTERRACIAL PROBLEMS OF AN
INTERRACIAL MOVEMENT

After this sketchy appraisal of organizational possibilities among various groups of the American poor, the question of an interracial movement must be taken up more directly.

We hope for a movement of all the poor, at a time when the Negro community is creating the only major movement in American society. The problems inherent in this situation are several and sensitive. We realize they will not be settled on paper, but only in actual work. Nevertheless it is critically necessary to state at least what the problems seem to be about.

The first is that in a very few instances are *any* white persons demonstrating a commitment to Negro causes, and in almost no instance is there actual evidence that *poor* whites can be mobilized. This makes it seem unfair to ask that the Negro movement take up economic issues as well as the directly racial issues which burden it today.

The second is that if whites *were* mobilized somehow, they would not represent an unambiguous sign of hope to the Negro movement. This is because many Negroes believe, with excellent historical justification, that the whites would dominate the movement and eventually receive the social rewards. This attitude is sharpened by the growing "black" ideologies of the new militant middle-class Negro leadership. These ideologies variously require Negro control of the Negro organizations, Negro staffs in the field, and a program of specific hostility to the whites of all classes. The usual psychological justification for such a program is the need to expunge alleged pent-up hatred of the Negro masses for the white man, either as a way to keep people moving or as a way to force action out of white society. Many integrationist ideologies, held by Negroes and whites, agree on the need for control and much of the time on the need for Negro staffs, while opposing the antiwhite features of the program wherever it might permanently alienate whites and Negroes who live in the same class circumstances.

The third problem is that the issues are not always conscious matters of debate, but they arise in the form of emotional tensions between people and organizations within the movement.

What are the arguments *for* an interracial movement?

1. The alternative is more likely to be fascism than freedom. We are not convinced that violent conflict between Negroes and lower-class whites will force the American establishment to even make significant concessions, much less

dissolve itself. The establishment might merely ignore the trouble and leave it to the local police, or it might use troops to enforce order. In either case, poor Negroes and poor whites will continue to struggle against each other instead of against the power structure that properly deserves their malice.

2. Since the Negroes are today the most *experienced* force for change, it is doubtful that they will fall to the rear of a movement of the poor. In generations gone by, the Irish, Italians, Jews, and other ethnic minorities rose to the partial security of the establishment through a labor movement and political machines which subordinated Negroes. That was an unforgivable action. But the process is not inevitable; it depends on the balance of forces at any one time. Today it seems inconceivable that Negroes would put up with less than a central role in directing the movement. Quite the contrary; would they not have *leading* roles in an interracial movement if their own action fosters it?

3. The economic problems of the Negro are class problems. They cannot be solved by the elimination of discrimination. The creation of decent housing, education, and employment requires massive change. No such massive change could improve the poor white without improving the life of the poor Negro. Some argue that the economic "solution" for the Negroes lies in compensatory treatment, or a "Marshall Plan for Negroes." This is quite true, and should be done, but it cannot compensate for joblessness except with a job—and there will not be enough jobs until there is a political movement that successfully demands them or, alternatively, a guaranteed income, from the government. Private business is not creating them and will not create them.

4. The psychological argument that the Negro must expunge hate is questionable on several grounds. It presumes that hate can be liberated while other feelings, such as kindness or openness, are suppressed, whereas it is doubtful that any such mechanical process exists. But even were the psyche to operate in this way, the strategy of liberating

hate begs two questions: First, is it morally justifiable to want to liberate hate alone? And, second, after the liberation of hate, how will the living conditions of lower-class Negroes improve?

These questions convince us of the need for a loose alliance of some kind, however difficult. In this context, we should approach the problem of the new Negro leaders and black ideologies more directly. We believe that the Negro community should be, and is, the main repository of guidance over the Negro movement. We believe that a racially-integrated staff legitimately should use the criterion of race in tactical and strategic decisions about organizing. We believe that much of the racial tension within the movement is rooted in our initial refusal to decide upon and maintain a *staff* policy of racial equality. Finally, we believe that the black ideology alone is incapable of leading to improvements in the everyday living conditions of Negro people. It can be one vital way of stirring people into participation, but it cannot eliminate poverty. The elimination of poverty, we think, requires the mobilization of all the power of the 75

to 100 million Americans who suffer it or suffer over it.

This is the same case we would take to the whites. . . . The whites must be organized on economic issues which are more important than their racial ideology. Perhaps today this is more possible than in the past because it is hard to imagine the poor white improving his economic condition without confronting a Negro movement already involved in many of the same issues. In this situation we think whites would decide to identify with the Negro struggle were it generally parallel to their own. Of course, the whites could opt for prejudice and further poverty—then we all lose. Whether this choice is made, perhaps, depends in large part on the organizational role we play.

This discussion no doubt will continue, and will be painful to us all. It should not become more important to argue than to organize, however, for only in organizing will the proof be found. So it is organizing we intend to do. Too many people are hungry and kept down, and we are mad. The question that remains is *how*.

HOW A MINORITY CAN CHANGE SOCIETY

George Breitman

In discussing the structural and cultural conditions obstructing black political action, George Breitman, a free-lance writer, raises considerations of black heritage, black economic position in the production apparatus, and black consciousness of the potential for change. In a spirit of optimism, often unchecked by reality, he asks when and how blacks can change their situation of oppression. What are the limitations on force and violence, on social dislocation? How is the white majority to be shown that black demands will benefit the entire society? What role does electoral politics play in all of this?

Before proceeding to our examination from a Marxist point of view of how

much and not how little a minority can do, I should make clear that I am not

From George Breitman, *How a Minority Can Change Society* (New York: Merit Publishers, 1964), pp. 16–26. Reprinted with permission of the publishers.

talking about just any minority, but but about a minority with certain characteristics, certain features, and a certain history. And also, yes, I am talking about a minority of a certain size. Let me get the size question out of the way first.

Obviously, not every minority is big enough to do the things I am talking about. Size is important too. If there were only two or three million Negroes in this country, which is approaching a population of 200 million, they could not accomplish what a minority of 20 million can. But 20 million is a big force, big enough to tear things up, big enough and weighty enough to appreciably affect the course of events. After all, how many countries in the world, not only the new ones in Africa and Asia but also the old ones in Europe and the Americas, have a population of 20 million? Out of more than 100 countries, not more than 25 at the most, so that around three-quarters of the countries in the world are smaller in population than the Negro people of the United States.

Size and relative weight are not the only important factors to be considered. A minority of even 40 million cannot do much if satisfied with its conditions or indifferent and apathetic about them. As important as size, or more important, in deciding what a minority can do are social, economic, political, historical, and psychological factors.

What I am trying to say is that what a minority can do depends on whether or not it is oppressed and exploited because of some minority trait or feature, is separated out by society for special inferior status, is denied equal treatment, opportunity and rights; whether or not it is at the bottom of the social ladder so that when it rises it shakes the whole structure; whether or not it is a part of the most productive and potentially most powerful force in the modern world, the working class, and yet at the same time is denied the full benefits of membership in that class; whether or not the oppressive and exploitative society in which it exists is stable or in crisis, challenged on all sides and therefore no longer able to maintain the

status quo; whether or not this minority believes that it can take advantage of the crisis of society; whether or not it is affected by and responds to the great tides of change and revolution sweeping the globe and has a sense of kinship and solidarity with the masses rising up and changing the rest of the world; whether or not its oppression tends to knit it together for common action and goals; whether or not it is compact and so situated geographically that it can act with maximum cohesiveness and impact; whether or not it has learned to see through the brainwashing which the ruling class uses to keep this minority in subjugation; whether or not it has lost patience as well as respect for the majority; whether or not it sees any further reason to continue believing in promises or in gradualism; whether or not it has the capacity to free itself from the influence of conservative leaders who have always held it back and to replace them with more militant and revolutionary leaders; whether or not it realizes it never has made any gains except by fighting for them; whether or not it has the capacity to defend itself against terror and violence; whether or not it is developing a militant and radical consciousness, ideology, philosophy and methodology of its own that can motivate and spark sustained, audacious and independent struggle.

In short, I am talking about characteristics that fit the American Negro people or which they are in the process of acquiring at an extremely rapid rate. Of the many things such a minority can do, I shall now list some, not necessarily in the order of their importance:

WHAT A MINORITY CAN DO

1. It can force serious concessions from the ruling class. Anyone who expects the capitalist class to grant full and genuine equality to the Negro people is going to be sadly disappointed, because equality is simply not compatible with, or possible under, a social system of the type that we have in the United States today. But that is no reason for Negroes to stop trying to get whatever they can squeeze out of the ruling class

until the time comes when it can be deposed. Militant struggle can force the present ruling class to lift some of the existing racial restrictions and barriers in the form of more rights, more jobs, better jobs, better schools, better housing, less police brutality, and a greater measure of formal equality before the law. Negroes will not settle for such partial gains and concessions, but they would be fools not to fight for them and take them and utilize them to press for other and more fundamental changes.

2. A minority, properly oriented and led, can go much farther than it has thus far gone to make the present system unworkable and intolerable. Bayard Rustin calls this "social dislocation" (and warns against its "limitations"). Rev. Albert Cleage, chairman of the Freedom Now Party in Michigan, calls it "a strategy of chaos" (and urges its application be expanded). Others give it the name of "mass civil disobedience." Whatever you call it, it has barely been utilized in America up to now. It consists of making the system so inconvenient and expensive that white people will be forced to ask themselves whether continued discrimination is worthwhile and whether in their own interest they should not help to do away with it altogether.

It means lying down, interposing your bodies on the airport runways, on the expressways, at the plant gate, at the school entrance, at the bank, at the points of production, and the points of distribution, and the points of transportation, and throwing a monkey wrench into the wheels of the system, attempting to paralyze it, to bring it to a stop. It means saying: "If we Negroes can't have decent and equal schools, then let's not have any schools. If we can't have jobs and job equality, then let no one be able to work. If we can't vote, then let no one be able to vote. If we can't belong to the unions as equals, then we don't care what happens to the unions." It means carrying the principle of the sit-down strike, which stops production, much farther and into entirely new areas of social life.

. . . The sit-ins, the lie-ins, the wade-ins, etc., were just a small, faint, preliminary version of what is still to come in a giant size and to the accomplishment of deep social convulsions and conflicts. To avoid misunderstanding, let me say that what I am talking about here is not pacifism but an all-out struggle, which will be the equivalent of a general strike when it reaches full flower. And a general strike usually tends to pose questions about who shall have power in the land.

3. A minority can, merely by carrying through its fight for democratic rights without compromise, help to educate and radicalize the American people, especially the youth in whose hands the future lies. In fact, it is already doing so. You in this audience of young socialists and young radicals know better than anyone else how profoundly your thinking about the whole world has been influenced by the Negro struggle; how their fight for equality enabled you to see through the official myths about "democracy" and "the free world," to understand the brute reality of the capitalist power structure, to reach new conclusions about capitalism and socialism. Not only the Cuban revolution, not only the danger of atomic war, but something much closer to home, the Negro revolt, has helped to educate or re-educate you, to shed the blinders of liberalism, and to persuade you to dedicate your lives to the fight for a better world. In this respect you are not so much unique as early, because the deepening struggle of the Negro minority will have similarly healthy effects on other young people and on some of the not completely hopeless older people as well.

POWER OF EXAMPLE

4. A minority not only can educate other forces but can set them into motion too. It can stimulate them to fight for their own needs and interests through the power of example as well as the power of pressure. You heard one illustration of the power of example this morning—the report about the rent strike which began among Negroes in Harlem and is now [1964] spreading to some white sections of the population

in other parts of New York City. Another small but striking example occurred in Detroit last summer. A militant Negro demonstration in front of police headquarters, to protest the police shooting of a young Negro woman in the back, came to the very brink of a physical clash. That was a Saturday, and it was followed two days later, on Monday, by another demonstration at another police station, near which cops had shot a young white man in the back. This second demonstration, involving mainly young whites, *raised the same slogans as the first* and culminated in a pitched battle with the cops after the youths had thrown rocks and bottles at them. Not long ago I noted a small newspaper item about some airline strike pickets who had been picketing up and down outside the Newark terminal for a long time, with little public attention paid to their grievances. One day they suddenly decided to go inside the terminal and demonstrate there, which was prohibited by an injunction. Quickly arrested, they were asked what had got into them. Their explanation was that they had seen that Negroes were able to get action by sit-ins and by going places where they weren't supposed to, so they thought it was a good idea to do the same.

These are all small-scale illustrations, but bigger and better ones are in the offing. The rulers of this country are well aware of the stimulation-and-contagion effects of militant Negro struggle. That is one reason why they want to stop it before it goes too far and explains the hasty turnabout that induced the previously indifferent Kennedy administration to suddenly introduce civil rights legislation last year.

5. A determined minority can also divide the majority, can actually split it up at decisive moments and junctures. This, of course, is one of the best ways of reducing the disadvantages of being a numerical minority, because it drastically changes the odds against the minority. The Socialist Workers party's 1963 convention resolution* showed

* *Freedom Now: The New Stage in the Struggle for Negro Emancipation,* Pioneer Publishers, 25¢.

how this process has operated historically. If our analysis and theory are correct, this isn't a matter of history only but of the present and the future. Let me refer briefly to the Civil War as an example of the process which can split the majority.

The Civil War was not just a conflict between abstract and impersonal forces, between Northern capitalism and Southern slavery; it was a struggle between classes and living people. No one played a greater role in stimulating and progressively resolving that conflict than the slaves and ex-slaves. Again and again in the three decades before the Civil War the rulers of the North and the South decided to avoid a final showdown by compromising over the slave question. Great hopes were raised and brilliant reputations were made overnight by these eminently "reasonable" negotiations and agreements reached over the bargaining table in Congress and then enacted into law. But the slaves were not consulted about these great compromises. They would not have consented to them anyway, because they left the condition of the slave unchanged, that is, intolerable. So the slaves continued their own independent efforts to become free, just as if these great compromise agreements had never existed.

HOW SLAVES FOUGHT

They continued, just as before, or more so, to run away by the thousands and tens of thousands, to commit sabotage and arson, and to engage in various forms of civil disobedience, self-defense and insurrection. These independent actions of the slaves helped to prevent the compromises from working and to stimulate the birth and growth of abolitionism among whites, who threw their weight onto the scales against further compromise. Thus the slaves reopened and widened the gap between the South and the North every time the great compromise statesmen tried to close it.

By acting in every way they could to defend and liberate themselves, the slaves drove a wedge between the slaveholders and those who wanted to compromise with the slaveholders. By acting in self-interest, and alone when they had to, the slaves divided the whites politically and morally and deepened the divisions to the breaking point. That, above everything else, is what made the struggle irrepressible, constantly widened the breach and deepened the division among the whites, and led inexorably to civil warfare. And then, at the crucial moment, after the outbreak of the war the rulers on both sides had tried so hard to avert, the Negroes pressured the northern government into accepting a revolutionary emancipation policy and completed the process by providing what the reluctant Lincoln later admitted was the military balance of power in the war itself. All this happened without a conscious plan, you might say instinctively. Imagine what will happen when the Negro militants absorb this lesson from history and then consciously work out a strategy to fully utilize this process that is set in motion by the elemental desire of the masses to be free!

We can expect, we can be certain, that the deepening of the Negro struggle for equality will have similarly divisive effects on the white majority in our own time. The majority is not homogeneous anyway: it is strained and torn and in conflict over a thousand questions of policy and class interest. A skillful leadership of the Negro minority will know how to pick the right place to drive new wedges, to deepen already existing and potential differences among the whites, to sharpen their conflicts, to set them fighting each other, and, in the process, as the SWP 1963 convention resolution also says, to find mutually beneficial alliances with those classes and forces whose interests are closer to those of the Negroes against those forces that are most hostile to the Negroes.

Under certain conditions, therefore, a minority, just by fighting for its own rights, can divide the majority into two or more minorities locked in combat with each other. This in turn can result in bringing to power a different kind of majority, not based on color, in which the original minority can take a leading part.

Those who confine themselves to scratching the surface can see only the limitations of being a minority, which leads to lamentation, pessimism, and self-induced paralysis or subservience. But when we examine the situation in all of its complex and contradictory reality, probing it deeper and from all sides; when we study majority-minority relations in motion as well as when they are standing still; when we perceive that the majority has problems too, and weaknesses, and many points at which it is vulnerable and susceptible to successful attack, and that these majority problems and weaknesses are becoming more acute than ever before, then we find, not just limitations for the minority, but also infinitely varied and promising openings and opportunities for transforming, transcending, and overcoming limitations.

POLITICAL POWER

6. The Negro minority is also in a position to upset the whole political structure of this country—just by "going it alone" in politics, just by the decisions Negroes make about how to use their own votes and their own minority political strength. Our 1963 convention resolution explored this question too, before the present Freedom Now party was started, but it bears restatement because it is such an effective refutation of black liberals who contend the Negro is politically impotent and "destined to fail" if he acts on his own in politics.

Negroes can form their own party. Negroes can run their own candidates against the Democrats and Republicans. Negroes, because they are already a majority in many districts, thanks to the segregated housing system that jams them tightly together in the big city ghettos, can, right now or any time they form their own party, elect dozens of black candidates to Congress from these districts and hundreds of state and local representatives. In this way they can get representatives in public office who will be responsible and accountable to the Negro community instead of to the corrupt major party machines. And since this bloc of black representatives will not be small, it will enable them to hold and wield a certain legislative balance

of power and to compel bigger concessions from the power structure than the
tokens and crumbs they are now thrown;
all of this, you notice, without any drastic change yet in political relations—
just by taking advantage of the political
and electoral conditions created by segregation, by refusing to vote Democratic
or Republican, by voting black. This
would mark a real advance at least in
the number and quality of Negro representatives in office, but that would be
only a part of the result of independent
political action.

By forming their own party, Negroes
can paralyze the Democratic party and
rock the whole political structure to its
foundations. Without Negro votes, the
bell will toll the doom of the Democratic
party. Without Negro votes, the Democratic coalition with the labor movement
will be undermined and destroyed.
Without Negro votes for that coalition,
the unions will be forced to reconsider
their political orientation, and this will
encourage and strengthen the union
forces who will eventually form an independent labor party. Without Negro
votes, the present two-party system will
pass from the scene and be replaced by
something different, out of which Negroes may be able to acquire new and
more reliable allies than up to now. And
all of this can be accomplished by the
simple device of forming a Negro party
and running independent Negro candidates. Really, when you think about the
potential, you can almost pity the igno-
rance of those Negro leaders who preach
that Negroes are incapable of any political role other than tagging along behind
the liberals.

7. The last on my partial list of things
the Negro minority can do should be of
special interest to another and smaller
minority—socialists, white and Negro.
I am convinced that if other Negroes
not yet socialist, are not so concerned
with this point now, they will be later
as their continuing political experience
draws it to their attention. At any rate,
my point is that the Negro people, although a minority, can, with consistently
revolutionary leadership, lead the American working class in the revolution that
will abolish capitalism.

We have long held the view that
while the Negro struggle is the struggle
of an oppressed minority for democratic
rights, for equality, it tends, because the
masters of this country are both unwilling and unable to grant equality, to become part of the general movement of
the exploited and oppressed to abolish
capitalism and proceed toward socialism. In this tendency to pass over from
democratic to socialist goals, to pass beyond the capitalist framework that now
envelops it, the Negro struggle is similar
to the colonial struggles, which also take
off from democratic aims, such as independence and self-government, but
find themselves unable to attain those
democratic aims until they wrench the
capitalist boot from off their neck. The
Chinese call this process "the uninter-
rupted revolution," and Leon Trotsky
called it "the permanent revolution."
But that is not what I am discussing
here. What I am talking about now is
something else—the capacity of the Negro people to *lead* the working-class revolution to replace capitalism with socialism.

3 Black Power: Significance And Prospects

AN ADVOCATE OF BLACK POWER DEFINES IT

Charles V. Hamilton

Black Power, in form a slogan, has come in substance to reflect the diverse contents of the civil rights movement in its later stages. For some, it is part of the struggle for liberation that former colonial subjects are waging against their masters. For others, it is a psychological gambit for a redefinition of self—part of the search for identity. For still others, it is a form of Negritude, the romanticization of blackness and of things African. For Charles V. Hamilton, Professor of Government at Columbia University, it is a form of ethnic politics, a bid for economic and political power, and a way of channeling black rage and frustration. Examples of Black Power include: cooperatives of black farmers and producers, black consultant and marketing firms, black industries (hospitals, chemical corporations, textile firms, construction companies), black professional organizations (teachers, students, social workers, lawyers, doctors), black schools in black communities, and black politicians. By unifying and solidifying the race, Black Power is a counter to black alienation; it commits people to themselves, to their values, to their community, and to their institutions.

Black Power has many definitions and connotations in the rhetoric of race relations today. To some people, it is synonymous with premeditated acts of violence to destroy the political and economic institutions of this country. Others equate Black Power with plans to rid the civil-rights movement of whites who have been in it for years. The concept is understood by many to mean hatred of and separation from whites; it is associated with calling whites "honkies" and with shouts of "Burn, baby, burn!" Some understood it to be the use of pressure-group tactics in the accepted tradition of the American political process. And still others say that Black Power must be seen first of all as an attempt to instill a sense of identity and pride in black people.

Ultimately, I suspect, we have to accept the fact that, in this highly charged atmosphere, it is virtually impossible to come up with a single definition satisfactory to all.

Even as some of us try to articulate our idea of Black Power and the way we relate to it and advocate it, we are categorized as "moderate" or "militant" or "reasonable" or "extremist." "I can

From *The New York Times*, VI, April 14, 1968, 21–23, 79–83. © 1968 by The New York Times Company. Reprinted by permission. Also by permission of the author.

accept your definition of Black Power," a listener will say to me. "But how does your position compare with what Stokely Carmichael said in Cuba or with what H. Rap Brown said in Cambridge, Md.?" Or, just as frequently, some young white New Left advocate will come up to me and proudly announce: "You're not radical enough. Watts, Newark, Detroit— that's what's happening, man! You're nothing but a reformist. We've got to blow up this society. Read Ché or Debray or Mao." All I can do is shrug and conclude that some people believe that making a revolution in this country involves rhetoric, Molotov cocktails and being under 30.

To have Black Power equated with calculated acts of violence would be very unfortunate. First, if black people have learned anything over the years, it is that he who shouts revolution the loudest is one of the first to run when the action starts. Second, open calls to violence are a sure way to have one's ranks immediately infiltrated. Third—and this is as important as any reason—violent revolution in this country would fail; it would be met with the kind of repression used in Sharpeville, South Africa, in 1960, when 67 Africans were killed and 186 wounded during a demonstration against apartheid. It is clear that America is not above this. There are many white bigots who would like nothing better than to embark on a program of black genocide, even though the imposition of such repressive measures would destroy civil liberties for whites as well as for blacks. Some whites are so panicky, irrational and filled with racial hatred that they would welcome the opportunity to annihilate the black community. This was clearly shown in the senseless murder of Dr. Martin Luther King Jr., which understandably—but nonetheless irrationally— prompted some black militants to advocate violent retaliation. Such cries for revenge intensify racial fear and animosity when the need—now more than ever—is to establish solid, stable organizations and action programs.

Many whites will take comfort in these words of caution against violence.

But they should not. The truth is that the black ghettos are going to continue to blow up out of sheer frustration and rage, and no amount of rhetoric from professors writing articles in magazines (which most black people in the ghettos do not read anyway) will affect that. There comes a point beyond which people cannot be expected to endure prejudice, oppression and deprivation, and they *will* explode.

Some of us can protect our positions by calling for "law and order" during a riot, or by urging "peaceful" approaches, but we should not be confident that we are being listened to by black people legitimately fed up with intolerable conditions. If white America wants a solution to the violence in the ghettos by blacks, then let white America end the violence done to the ghettos by whites. We simply must come to understand that there can be no social order without social justice. "How long will the violence in the summers last?" another listener may ask. "How intransigent is white America?" is my answer. And the answer to that could be just more rhetoric or it could be a sincere response to legitimate demands.

Black Power must not be naive about the intentions of white decision-makers to yield anything without a struggle and a confrontation by organized power. Black people will gain only as much as they can win through their ability to organize independent bases of economic and political power—through boycotts, electoral activity, rent strikes, work stoppages, pressure-group bargaining. And it must be clear that whites will have to bargain with blacks or continue to fight them in the streets of the Detroits and the Newarks. Rather than being a call to violence, this is a clear recognition that the ghetto rebellions, in addition to producing the possibility of apartheid-type repression, have been functional in moving *some* whites to see that viable solutions must be sought.

Black Power is concerned with organizing the rage of black people and with putting new, hard questions and demands to white America. As we do this, white America's responses will be crucial to the questions of violence and viability. Black Power must (1) deal with the obviously growing alienation of black people and their distrust of the institutions of this society; (2) work to create new values and to build a new sense of community and of belonging, and (3) work to establish legitimate new institutions that make participants, not recipients, out of a people traditionally excluded from the fundamentally racist processes of this country. There is nothing glamorous about this; it involves persistence and hard, tedious, day-to-day work.

Black Power rejects the lessons of slavery and segregation that caused black people to look upon themselves with hatred and disdain. To be "integrated" it was necessary to deny, one's heritage, one's own culture, to be ashamed of one's black skin, thick lips and kinky hair. In their book, "Racial Crisis in America," two Florida State University sociologists, Lewis M. Killian and Charles M. Grigg, wrote: "At the present time, integration as a solution to the race problem demands that the Negro forswear his identity as a Negro. But for a lasting solution, the meaning of 'American' must lose its implicit racial modifier, 'white.' " The black man must change his demeaning conception of himself; he must develop a sense of pride and self-respect. Then, if integration comes, it will deal with people who are psychologically and mentally healthy, with people who have a sense of their history and of themselves as whole human beings.

In the process of creating these new values, Black Power will, its advocates hope, build a new sense of community among black people. It will try to forge a bond in the black community between those who have "made it" and those "on the bottom." It will bring an end to the internal back-biting and suspicious bickering, the squabbling over tactics and personalities so characteristic of the black community. If Black Power can produce this unity, that in itself will be revolutionary, for the black community and for the country.

Black Power recognizes that new forms of decision-making must be implemented in the black community. One purpose, clearly, is to overcome the alienation and distrust.

Let me deal with this specifically by looking at the situation in terms of "internal" and "external" ghetto problems and approaches. When I speak of internal problems, I refer to such things as exploitative merchants who invade the black communities, to absentee slumlords, to inferior schools and arbitrary law enforcement, to black people unable to develop their own independent economic and political bases. There are, of course, many problems facing black people which must be dealt with outside the ghettos: jobs, open occupancy, medical care, higher education.

The solution of the internal problems does not require the presence of massive numbers of whites marching arm in arm with blacks. Local all-black groups can organize boycotts of disreputable merchants and of those employers in the black communities who fail to hire and promote black people. Already, we see this approach spreading across the country with Operation Breadbasket, initiated by Dr. King's Southern Christian Leadership Conference. The national director of the program, the Rev. Jesse Jackson, who was with Dr. King when he was murdered in Memphis, has established several such projects from Los Angeles to Raleigh, N.C.

In Chicago alone, in 15 months, approximately 2,000 jobs worth more than $15-million in annual income were obtained for black people. Negotiations are conducted on hiring and upgrading black people, marketing the products of black manufacturers and suppliers and providing contracts to black companies. The operation relies heavily on the support of black businessmen, who are willing to work with Operation Breadbasket because it is mutually beneficial. They derive a profit and in turn contribute to the economic development of the black community.

This is Black Power in operation. But there is not nearly enough of this kind of work going on. In some instances, there is a lack of technical know-how coupled with a lack of adequate funds. These two defects constantly plague constructive pressure-group activity in the black communities.

CORE (Congress of Racial Equality) has developed a number of cooperatives around the country. In Opelousas, La., it has organized over 300 black farmers, growers of sweet potatoes, cabbages and okra, in the Grand-Marie Co-op. They sell their produce and some of the income goes back into the co-op as dues. Initially, 20 per cent of the cooperative's members were white farmers, but most of the whites dropped out as a result of social and economic pressures from the white community. An offshoot of the Grand-Marie group is the Southern Consumers' Cooperative in Lafayette, La., which makes and sells fruit cakes and candy. It has been in existence for more than a year, employs approximately 150 black people and has led to the formation of several credit unions and buying clubs.

The major effort of Black Power-oriented CORE is in the direction of economic development. Antoine Perot, program director of CORE, says: "One big need in the black community is to develop capital-producing instruments which create jobs. Otherwise, we are stuck with the one-crop commodity—labor—which does not produce wealth. Mere jobs are not enough. These will simply perpetuate black dependency."

Thus, small and medium-sized businesses are being developed in the black communities of Chicago, San Francisco, Detroit, Cleveland, New York and several other urban centers. CORE hopes to call on some successful black businessmen around the country as consultants, and it is optimistic that they will respond favorably with their know-how and, in some instances, their money. The goal is to free as many black people as possible from economic dependency on the white man. It has been this dependency in many places that has hampered effective independent political organizing.

In New York, Black Power, in the way we see it, operates through a group called N.E.G.R.O. (National Economic Growth and Reconstruction Organization). Its acronym does not sit too well with some advocates of black consciousness who see in the use of the term "Negro" an indication of less than sufficient racial pride. Started in 1964, the group deals with economic self-help for the black community: a hospital in Queens, a chemical corporation, a textile company and a construction company. N.E.G.R.O., with an annual payroll of $1 million and assets of $3 million, is headed by Dr. Thomas W. Matthew, a neurosurgeon who has been accused of failing to file Federal income-tax returns for 1961, 1962 and 1963. He has asserted that he will pay all the Government says he owes, but not until "my patient is cured or one of us dies." His patient is the black community, and the emphasis of his group is on aiding blacks and reducing reliance on the white man. The organization creates a sense of identity and cohesiveness that is painfully lacking in much of the black community.

In helping oneself and one's race through hard work, N.E.G.R.O. would appear to be following the Puritan ethic of work and achievement: if you work hard, you will succeed. One gets the impression that the organization is not necessarily idealistic about this. It believes that black people will never develop in this country as long as they must depend on handouts from the white man. This is realism, whatever ethic it is identified with. And this, too, is Black Power in operation.

More frequently than not, projects will not use the term "Black Power," but that is hardly necessary. There is, for instance, the Poor People's Corporation, formed by a former S.N.C.C. (Student Non-violent Coordinating Committee) worker, Jessie Norris, in August, 1965. It has set up 15 cooperatives in Mississippi, employing about 200 black people. The employes, all shareholders, make handbags, hats, dresses, quilts, dolls and other hand-craft items that are marketed through Liberty House in Jackson, Miss. Always sensitive to the development of the black community, the Poor People's Corporation passed a rule that only registered voters could work in the co-ops.

These enterprises are small; they do not threaten the economic structure of this society, but their members look upon them as vital for the development of the black people. Their purpose is to establish a modicum of economic self-sufficiency without focusing too much attention on the impact they will have on the American economic system.

Absolutely crucial to the development of Black Power is the black middle class. These are people with sorely needed skills. There has been a lot of discussion about where the black middle class stands in relation to Black Power. Some people adopt the view that most members of the class opt out of the race (or at least try to do so); they get good jobs, a nice home, two cars, and forget about the masses of blacks who have not "made it." This has been largely true. Many middle-class blacks simply do not feel an obligation to help the less fortunate members of their race.

There is, however, a growing awareness among black middle-class people of their role in the black revolution. On Jan. 20, a small group of them (known, appropriately enough, as the Catalysts) called an all-day conference in a South Side Chicago church to discuss ways of linking black middle-class professionals with black people in the lower class. Present were about 370 people of all sorts: teachers, social workers, lawyers, accountants, three physicians, housewives, writers. They met in workshops to discuss ways of making their skills and positions relevant to the black society, and they held no press conferences. Though programs of action developed, the truth is that they remain the exception, not the rule, in the black middle class.

Another group has been formed by black teachers in Chicago, Detroit and New York, and plans are being made to expand. In Chicago, the organization is called the Association of Afro-American Educators. These are people who have traditionally been the strongest support-

ers of the status quo. Education is intended to develop people who will support the existing values of the society, and "Negro" teachers have been helping this process over the years. But now some of them (more than 250 met on Feb. 12 in Chicago) are organizing and beginning to redefine, first, their role as black educators vis-à-vis the black revolution, and, second, the issues as they see them. Their motivation is outlined in the following statement:

"By tapping our vast resources of black intellectual expertise, we shall generate new ideas for *meaningful* educational programs, curricula and instructional materials which will contribute substantially toward raising the educational achievement of black children.

"Our purpose is to extricate ourselves momentarily from the dominant society in order to realign our priorities, to mobilize and to 'get ourselves together' to do what must be done by those best equipped to do it."

This is what they *say;* whether they can pull it off will depend initially on their ability to bring along their black colleagues, many of whom, admittedly, do not see the efficacy of such an attitude. Unless the link is made between the black middle-class professionals and the black masses, Black Power will probably die on the speaker's platform.

Another important phenomenon in the development of Black Power is the burgeoning of black students' groups on college campuses across the country. I have visited 17 such campuses—from Harvard to Virginia to Wisconsin to U.C.L.A.—since October. The students are discussing problems of identity, of relevant curricula at their universities, of ways of helping their people when they graduate. Clearly, one sees in these hundreds (the figure could be in the thousands) of black students a little bit of Booker T. Washington (self-help and the dignity of common labor) and a lot of W. E. B. DuBois (vigorous insistence on equality and the liberal education of the most talented black men).

These are the people who are planning to implement social, political and economic Black Power in their home towns. They will run for public office, aware that Richard Hatcher started from a political base in the black community. He would not be Mayor of Gary, Ind., today if he had not first mobilized the black voters. Some people point out that he had to have white support. This is true; in many instances such support is necessary, but internal unity is necessary first.

This brings us to a consideration of the external problems of the black community. It is clear that black people will need the help of whites at many places along the line. There simply are not sufficient economic resources—actual or potential—in the black community for a total, unilateral, boot-strap operation. Why should there be? Black people have been the target of deliberate denial for centuries, and racist America has done its job well. This is a serious problem that must be faced by Black Power advocates. On the one hand, they recognize the need to be independent of "the white power structure." And on the other, they must frequently turn to that structure for help—technical and financial. Thus, the rhetoric and the reality often clash.

Resolution probably lies in the realization by white America that it is in her interest not to have a weak, dependent, alienated black community inhabiting the inner cities and blowing them up periodically. Society needs stability, and as long as there is a sizable powerless, restless group within it which considers the society illegitimate, stability is not possible. However it is calculated, the situation calls for a black-white rapprochement, which may well come only through additional confrontations and crises. More frequently than not, the self-interest of the dominant society is not clearly perceived until the brink is reached.

There are many ways whites can relate to this phenomenon. First, they must recognize that blacks are going to insist on an equitable distribution of *decision-making power*. Anything less will simply be perpetuating a welfare mentality among blacks. And if the so-

ciety thinks only in terms of *giving* more jobs, better schools and more housing, the result will be the creation of more black recipients still dependent on whites.

The equitable distribution of power must result from a conviction that it is a matter of mutual self-interest, not from the feelings of guilt and altruism that were evident at the National Conference of New Politics convention in Chicago in August [1967]. An equitable distribution means that black men will have to occupy positions of political power in precincts, counties, Congressional districts and cities where their numbers and organization warrant. It means the end of absentee white ward committeemen and precinct captains in Chicago's black precincts.

But this situation is much easier described than achieved. Black Americans generally are no more likely to vote independently than other Americans. In many Northern urban areas, especially, the job of wooing the black vote away from the Democratic party is gigantic. The established machine has the resources: patronage, tradition, apathy. In some instances the change will take a catalytic event—a major racial incident, a dramatic black candidate, a serious boner by the white establishment (such as splitting the white vote). The mere call to "blackness" simply is not enough, even where the numbers are right.

In addition, many of the problems facing black people can be solved only to the extent that whites are willing to see such imperatives as an open housing market and an expanding job market. White groups must continue to bring as much pressure as possible on local and national decision-makers to adopt sound policy in these fields. These enlightened whites *will* be able to work with Black Power groups.

There are many things which flow from this orientation to Black Power. It is not necessary that blacks create parallel agencies—political or economic—in all fields and places. In some areas, it is possible to work within, say, the two-party system. Richard Hatcher did so in Gary, but he first had to organize black voters to fight the Democratic machine in the primary. The same is true of Mayor Carl Stokes in Cleveland. At some point it may be wise to work with the existing agencies, but this must be done only from a base of independent, not subordinated, power.

On the other hand, dealing with a racist organization like George Wallace's Democratic party in Alabama would require forming an independent group. The same is true with some labor unions, especially in the South, which still practice discrimination despite the condemnation of such a policy by their parent unions. Many union locals are willing to refuse to join the fight for open housing laws.

The point is that black people must become much more pragmatic in their approach. Whether we try to work within or outside a particular agency should depend entirely on a hard-nosed, calculated examination of potential success in each situation—a careful analysis of cost and benefit. Thus, when we negotiate the test will be: How will black people, not some political machine down town or some labor union boss across town, benefit from this?

Black Power must insist that the institutions in the black community be led by and, wherever possible, staffed by blacks. This is advisable psychologically, and it is necessary as a challenge to the myth that black people are incapable of leadership. Admittedly, this violates the principle of egalitarianism ("We hire on the basis of merit alone, not color"). What black and white America must understand is that egalitarianism is just a *principle* and it implies a notion of "color-blindness" which is deceptive. It must be clear by now that any society which has been color-conscious all its life to the detriment of a particular group cannot simply become color-blind and expect that group to compete on equal terms.

Black Power clearly recognizes the need to perpetuate color consciousness, but in a positive way—to improve a group, not to subject it. When principles like egalitarianism have been so flagrantly violated for so long, it does not make sense to think that the victim of that violation can be equipped to benefit from opportunities simply upon their pronouncement. Obviously, some positive form of special treatment must be used to overcome centuries of negative special treatment.

This has been the argument of the Nation of Islam (the so-called Black Muslims) for years; it has also been the position of the National Urban League since its proposal for preferential treatment (the Domestic Marshall Plan, which urged a "special effort to overcome serious disabilities resulting from historic handicaps") was issued at its 1963 Denver convention. This is not racism. It is not intended to penalize or subordinate another group; its goal is the positive uplift of a deliberately repressed group. Thus, when some Black Power advocates call for the appointment of black people to head community-action poverty programs and to serve as school principals, they have in mind the deliberate projection of blacks into positions of leadership. This is important to give other black people a feeling of ability to achieve, if nothing else. And it is especially important for young black children.

An example of concentrated special treatment is the plan some of us are proposing for a new approach to education in some of the black ghettos. It goes beyond the decentralization plans in the Bundy Report; it goes beyond the community involvement at I.S. 201 in Harlem. It attempts to build on the idea proposed by Harlem CORE last year for an independent Board of Education for Harlem.

Harlem CORE and the New York Urban League saw the Bundy Report as a "step toward creating a structure which would bring meaningful education to the children of New York." CORE, led by Roy Innis, suggested an autonomous Harlem school system, chartered by the State Legislature and responsible to the state. "It will be run by an elected school board and an appointed administrator, as most school boards are," CORE said. "The elected members will be Harlem residents. It is important that much of the detailed planning and structure be the work of the Harlem community." Funds would come from city, state and Federal governments and from private sources. In describing the long-range goal of the proposal, CORE says: "Some have felt it is to create a permanently separate educational system. Others have felt it is a necessary step toward eventual integration. In any case, the ultimate outcome of this plan will be to make it possible for Harlem to choose."

Some of us propose that education in the black community should be family-oriented, not simply child-oriented. In many of the vast urban black ghettos (which will not be desegregated in the foreseeable future) the school should become the focal point of the community. This we call the Family-Community-School-Comprehensive Plan. School would cease to be a 9-to-3, September-to-June, time-off-for-good-behavior institution. It would involve education and training for the entire family—all year round, day and evening. Black parents would be intimately involved as students, decision-makers, teachers. This is much more than a revised notion of adult education courses in the evening or the use of mothers as teachers' aides.

This plan would make the educational system the center of community life. We could have community health clinics and recreational programs built into the educational system. Above all, we could reorient the demeaning public welfare system, which sends caseworkers to "investigate" families. Why could we not funnel public assistance through the community educational program?

One major advantage would be the elimination of some of the bureaucratic chaos in which five to ten governmental agencies zero in on the black family on welfare, seldom if ever coordinating their programs. The welfare department, for one, while it would not need to be altered in other parts of the state, would have to work jointly with the educational system in the black community. This would obviously require administrative reorganization, which would not necessarily reduce bureaucracy but would consolidate and centralize it. In addition to being "investigators," for example, some caseworkers (with substantially reduced case loads) could become teachers of budgetary management, and family health consultants could report the economic needs of the family.

The teachers for such a system would be specially trained in a program similar to the National Teacher Corps, and recruits could include professionals as well as mothers who could teach classes in child-rearing, home economics, art, music or any number of skills they obviously possess. Unemployed fathers could learn new skills or teach the ones they know. The curriculum would be both academic and vocational, and it would contain courses in the culture and history of black people. The school would belong to the community. It would be a union of children, parents, teachers, social workers, psychologists, urban planners, doctors, community organizers. It would become a major vehicle for fashioning a sense of pride and group identity.

I see no reason why the local law-enforcement agency could not be integrated into this system. Perhaps this could take the form of training "community service officers," or junior policemen, as suggested in the report of the President's Commission on Civil Disorders. Or the local police precinct could be based in the school, working with the people on such things as crime prevention, first aid and the training of police officers. In this way, mutual trust could be developed between the black community and the police.

Coordinating these programs would present problems to be worked out on the basis of the community involved, the agencies involved and the size of the system. It seems quite obvious that in innovations of this sort there will be a tremendous amount of chaos and uncertainty and there will be mistakes. This is understandable; it is the price to be paid for social change under circumstances of widespread alienation and deprivation. The recent furor about the Malcolm X memorial program at I.S. 201 in Harlem offers an example of the kind f problem to be anticipated. Rather han worrying about what one person aid from a stage at a particular meet- ng, the authorities should be concerned about how the Board of Education will ooperate to transfer power to the community school board. When the transfer s made, confusion regarding lines of authority and program and curriculum content can be reduced.

The longer the delay in making the ransfer, however, the greater the likelihood of disruption. One can expect misunderstanding, great differences of opinion and a relatively low return on efforts at the beginning of such new programs. New standards of evaluation are being set, and the experimental concept developed at I.S. 201 should not be jeopardized by isolated incidents. It would be surprising if everything went smoothly from the outset.

Some programs *will* flounder, some will collapse out of sheer incompetence and faulty conception, but this presents an opportunity to build on mistakes. The precise details of the Comprehensive Plan would have to be worked out in conjunction with each community and agency involved. But the *idea* is seriously proposed. We must begin to think in entirely new terms of citizen involvement and decision-making.

Black power has been accused of emphasizing decentralization, of overlooking the obvious trend toward consolidation. This is not true with the kind of Black Power described here, which is ultimately not separatist or isolationist. Some Black Power advocates are aware that this country is simultaneously experiencing centralization and decentralization. As the Federal Government becomes more involved (and it must) in the lives of people, it is imperative that we broaden the base of citizen participation. It will be the new forms, new agencies and structures developed by Black Power that will link these centralizing and decentralizing trends.

Black Power structures at the local level will activate people, instill faith (not alienation) and provide a habit of organization and a consciousness of ability. Alienation will be overcome and trust in society restored. It will be through these local agencies that the centralized forces will operate, not through insensitive, unresponsive city halls. Billions of dollars will be needed each year, and these funds must be provided through a more direct route from their sources to the people.

Black Power is a developmental process; it cannot be an end in itself. To the extent that black Americans can organize, and to the extent that white Americans can keep from panicking and begin to respond rationally to the demands of that organization—to that extent can we get on with the protracted business of creating not just law and order but a free and open society.

BLACK POWER: A DISCUSSION

Tom Kahn

In the selection that follows, Tom Kahn, Executive Director of the League for Industrial Democracy, argues that Black Power needs to be more than a mere slogan—a grab bag for all diverse tendencies within the civil rights movement. He suggests that for the concept to have meaning, it must contain a program for massive social reform which will extend the integrative trends within that movement even further. Since riots and rebellions will not be tolerated, mechanisms of reform must be offered.

*In this spirit, he urges the radicalization of the present liberal coalition
and the cancelling out of those blacks and whites who are urging
segregated solutions which are futile, nihilistic gestures at best.*

Is it not remarkable that so much effort is devoted to the exegesis of a slogan? One would think the phrase "Black Power" had an independent existence, a substance and dynamic of its own. Yet words are presumably invented to indicate preexisting things; and at least in politics, slogans have typically arisen as popular condensations of preexisting ideas. (People may have disagreed on how "Bread and Land" or "Forty Acres and a Mule" or even "Freedom Now" were to be precisely achieved, but the idea was clear enough.) Now we have a slogan for which we must find meanings, a form in search of content. It is perhaps a sign of the times, this reversion to magical symbolism. The new route takes us beyond protest, around politics, to incantations.

In the beginning, of course, were Stokeley Carmichael and his followers chanting the words on the Mississippi March. Since then, "Black Power" has been echoed by different people for different reasons. What we should really be talking about is who these people are, what they want and how they propose to get it. These are the considerations that, interacting with the response of white America, will determine the actual, concrete meaning of "Black Power."

There is space here only for some assertions and a few comments on Martin Duberman's perceptive article.[1]

1. The ambiguity which Mr. Duberman notes in "Black Power" stems in my opinion less from press distortion of SNCC and CORE statements than from the slogan having become a grab-bag for diverse tendencies within the Negro

movement. (No doubt the mass media have not done justice to the full range and complexity of Rap Brown's philosophy; still, when his pronouncement on nearly every social problem is "Better get you some guns," little room is left for further distortion.) The difficulty is that "Black Power" now embraces: would-be guerrilla warriors *à la* Frantz Fanon and Che Guevara; advocates (in Christopher Lasch's words)[2] of "traditional 'nationalist' measures ranging from cooperative businesses to proposals for complete separation," many of whom are associated with CORE; various Negro intellectuals and professionals in whom the degree of integration we have achieved has induced an identity crisis; old-line politicians who see in "Black Power" a potential instrument for erecting or shoring up ghetto machines; small businessmen seeking to enter, preserve or expand all-black markets; preachers who have long held their black congregations together with sermons about self-help and "the chosen people"; artists, actors and entertainers who are exploring the Negro's history and culture for new forms of expression; etc.

2. Obviously, some facets of "Black Power" can be absorbed by this society; they conform with our tradition and value structure. In this category are the emphasis on self-help and the tacit acceptance of segregation. Other facets will be nominally accepted but really underminded. Thus, Negroes will be encouraged to open small businesses, while the trend will be toward more big business consolidation and domination; Negroes will be given increasing control over ghetto education and political machines, while the power and resources continue shifting to suburbia and the Federal government. Like Booker T.

[1] Martin Duberman, "Black Power and the American Radical Tradition," *Partisan Review*, XXXV (Winter 1968), 34–68. Duberman, attacking the separation and self-help attitudes of Black Power advocates, warned against an anarchist focus which flies in the face of the conformist and centralizing trends of contemporary society. [Editor's note.]

[2] Cf. Lasch's article on Black Power in Annotated Bibliography. [Editor's note.]

From *Partisan Review*, XXXV (Spring 1968), 210–216. © 1968 by Partisan Review. Reprinted by permission of the publisher and the author.

Washington, who urged Negroes to stay
in the South and acquire handicraft
skills when industrialization and urban-
zation were the national trends, some
Black Power" advocates may be described by future historians as Uncle
Toms.

Finally, there are the elements of
Black Power" that clearly cannot be
absorbed. Whether one sees the ghetto
uprisings as riots or rebellions, they will
be stopped. The right to overthrow a
government may be proclaimed by revolutionaries, but the right to suppress
rebellion is claimed and, more impor-
antly, exercised by governments. And
in the United States it would be suppressed with the support of the overwhelming majority of the population
and with a show of force commensurate
with the magnitude of the threat. If in
addition to violence and anti-white racism "Black Power" becomes identified
with Maoism, Castroism or support of
the Vietcong, the threat will loom plaus-
ibly larger in the sights of most Americans. How they react will ultimately
prove more important, like it or not,
than all the finely woven interpreta-
tions, redefinitions and elaborations of
"Black Power" now being offered. Unfortunately a democrat, no matter how
frustrated, cannot simply snub his nose
at the sluggish and benighted majority;
or, if he does he may win a few battles
but will surely lose the war.

3. Within "Black Power" we may find
a thousand subtle and tantalizing questions bearing on the human condition,
but the overriding question is what are
we going to do. And the fundamental
choice before us is this: will we undertake the massive social reform that is
required to make room for the Negro on
the basis of equality, or shall we rather
encourage the Negro community to turn
inward, seeking internal moral reforma-
tion and economic uplift within the
bounds of segregation?

The latter approach, incidentally, is
not only sanctioned by our traditions but
also lends itself precisely to the conservative piecemeal approach to social problems that characterizes the "pragmatic"
American spirit. Foundation grants can

substitute for social investment by government; planning can focus on clearly
delineated little neighborhood boxes, instead of on metropolitan and national
arrangements. The trouble with this, as
Mr. Duberman points out, is that "many
of the basic ills from which Negro-Amer-
icans suffer . . . are national phenomena
and require national resources to overcome," and that "whether these resources
will be allocated in sufficient amounts
will depend . . . on whether a national
coalition can be formed to exact pressure on the federal government. . . ."

4. What should be the character of
this coalition, and what forces should it
comprise? The Black Power advocates
feel, in Mr. Duberman's words, that "the
only kind of progressive coalition that
can exist in this country . . . is the mild,
liberal variety which produced the civil
rights legislation of recent years. And
that kind of legislation has proven itself
grossly inadequate." Mr. Duberman then
suggests that: "If a radical coalition
could be formed in this country, that is,
one willing to scrutinize in depth the
failings of our system, to suggest structural, not piecemeal, reforms, to see
them executed with sustained rather
than occasional vigor, then Black Power
advocates might feel less need to separate themselves and to concentrate on
local marginal successes. But no responsible observer believes that in the foreseeable future a radical coalition on the
Left can become the effective political
majority. . . ."

I want to concentrate on these statements and their implications because I
believe they explain, at least in part,
why Mr. Duberman's essay, like Christopher Lasch's also brilliant piece, "The
Trouble with Black Power," in *The New
York Review of Books*,[3] finally leaves me
unsatisfied. Rightly critical of the in-
adequacies of recent liberal legislation,
yet pessimistic as to radicalism's imme-

[3] Lasch speaks of the psychological cry of
congeries of colonial guerrillas, hell-bent to be
the vanguard of revolutionary change on the
American soil. He bemoans their romantic
anarchism, nihilism and lack of a political
program; but he is equally critical of reformist
solutions to the race crisis. [Editor's note.]

diate prospects, both writers deliver a surefire indictment of the society, then walk off leaving us stranded, with nowhere to turn. Maybe there is no place to turn, in which case the most incisive critiques of Black Power are pointless; if there are no serious alternatives, we might as well let everybody do his own thing. But I do not think we have reached this impasse.

Mr. Duberman lists several examples of the failures of the liberal legislation produced in recent years—e.g., despite the Supreme Court decision, 85 per cent of Negro students in the South are still in segregated schools; unemployment among Negroes has risen in the past decade; Title VI of the 1964 Civil Rights Act has been poorly enforced; and so has the 1965 Voting Rights Act. This is all true, and the list could be extended. But surely one cannot argue—although Mr. Duberman may underestimate the radical impact of the Voting Rights Act —that this list defines liberalism's program, that these results flow from liberalism. They flow rather from the frustration and undermining of liberal programs by an entrenched and now resurgent conservatism.

5. To recognize this does not mean that liberalism, if it were decisively to defeat conservatism, would be sufficient for all our problems. As a socialist, I do not believe that. But neither would I want to fall into the error of earlier radical movements that declared socialism the precondition for full employment, the elimination of Jim Crow and other goals now widely recognized as attainable under liberal capitalism. To assume that liberalism has spent itself when in fact it has not yet come into its own— for an array of historical reasons—is to establish a premise that can only lead radicalism into vastly mistaken strategies. For one thing, it confuses liberalism's ideals with what is left of them after their confrontation with conservatism. Simultaneously, radicalism claims for itself what liberalism promised before the confrontation. Radicalism becomes chaste liberalism or triumphant liberalism, instead of a qualitatively different politics.

In any case, I am not convinced tha a *radical* coalition, as desirable as tha surely is, is required to achieve what th liberal coalition has sought, but failed to achieve. If the liberal coalition, a powerful and respectable as it is, canno desegregate hospital facilities receivin federal funds, what hope is there at pres ent for a radical political majority in th United States? None, as Mr. Duberma says. From a premature breakdown o liberalism we are more apt to get reac tion than radicalism. Only as liberalisn triumphs over conservatism does radi calism become a relevant option.

Yet one finds among many New Left ists and some older intellectuals a kin of glee in viewing the fragmentation an weakening of the liberal coalition, as i a radical movement stood ready in th wings to take over. They see Vietnan as a crucible in which the excess fat o liberalism is boiled away, leaving har crystals of political purity—for tomor row. Of these people, as of SNCC an CORE, we may wonder with Mr. Duber man "whether they are really interestec in a future reconciliation." But whethe they are interested or not, political events are moving too rapidly for anyone to be confident of the political configurations two, five or ten years from now.

6. Radicals today should be working with and within the liberal coalition despite differences over Vietnam, for disintegration of the coalition will neither enhance the prospects of peace nor move us toward a more democratic foreign policy. Indeed the prospect of a more democratic foreign policy hinges largely on winning the mass domestic interest-based constituencies to the view that peace depends on the extension into international affairs of progressive social and economic policies at home. This process is not accelerated but retarded by a rhetoric which counterposes domestic and foreign policies by proclaiming that domestic social needs must await a peaceful settlement in Vietnam. Superficially this line appears to link domestic and foreign policy issues, but in reality it tends to isolate the Doves who employ it from the day-to-day struggles of those who cannot afford to wait

or peace in Vietnam or to transfer their energies exclusively to that end. It does no good to tell residents of the ghetto that the war in Vietnam makes help for them impossible, which is what the conservatives are saying. It makes more sense to say what is after all the truth: that the war provides only the latest in a long succession of phony conservative excuses for defaulting on the nation's promises.

The arguments of *The Freedom Budget*[4] persuade me that, with full utilization of our economic resources and with appropriate fiscal policies, this country can afford both a war in Vietnam, *should we choose to pursue it*, and a war on poverty. To argue the incompatibility of the two "wars" on economic grounds is to obscure a basic political issue: the resistance of the affluent middle classes to heavier taxation. The cutbacks in poverty programs are attributable less to Vietnam than to class relations and the way they influence the distribution of political power in the United States. These relations were not forged in Vietnam, and they will not be altered there. To focus on Vietnam as *the* obstacle (at least economically) to domestic progress is to let a lot of privileged people off the hook.

Meanwhile, I suspect that the same future historians who will see in "Black Power" a reversion to Booker T. Washington's philosophy will see an equally ironic parallel between those who today would tie the Negro's liberation to peace in Vietnam and those in the early Socialist movement who saw the "Negro question" as simply a phase in the class struggle. Like the case for the existence of the class struggle then, the case for a peaceful settlement in Vietnam now is sufficiently cogent without appending the "Negro question" as a tail to its kite. Now as then it is a question demanding attention and action in its own right.

7. Aside from the probability that this war, like most, tends to bring domestic violence to the surface, the Vietnam war has affected the ghetto more indirectly than directly. By dividing the liberal movement and giving excuses to the conservatives, it has made massive new programs less likely. And by intensifying feelings of powerlessness, alienation and guilt among many white liberals, it has increased their emotional vulnerability to the most extreme Black Power denunciations and accusations. (After all, if you are seriously entertaining the thought that the white American government is committing genocide in Vietnam, then it is not conceivable that. . . .)

It is by no means clear that the domestic stalemate will be broken when the war in Vietnam ends. A slowdown in the war on poverty and racism was evident before the Vietnam escalation, and the danger is that peace in Vietnam would bring added problems of employment and conversion with which the nation may not be politically prepared to cope. We have a better chance if the liberal coalition is still around and if it is united on a far-reaching program of social and economic reconstruction.

8. In this connection, I think Mr. Duberman makes a serious mistake in writing off the bulk of the organized labor movement, a practice which the Vietnam crisis has made all the more fashionable *Partisan Review* might someday consider a symposium analyzing the labor movement's foreign policy positions, but the fact is that right now the labor movement as-a whole—and not simply the UAW and the UFT—has by far the most advanced economic policies of any major institution in American life. This has the ring of a thirties' cliché, but it happens to be true, as anyone who takes the trouble to read the publications of the AFL-CIO or to familiarize himself with its legislative campaigns can easily discover. There is much to be criticized in the labor movement, but no liberal coalition with muscle and staying power can be constructed apart from it. Had the liberal intellectuals of recent years absorbed more of labor's concern with full employment, higher wages, expanded housing construction and increased federal spending for social pur-

---

[4] A *"Freedom Budget for All Americans: Budgeting Our Resources, 1966–1975, to Achieve "Freedom from Want"* (New York: A. Philip Randolph Institute, 1966). [Editor's note.]

poses, instead of so often portraying the nation's problems as cultural, legal and aesthetic, the gap between "white liberalism" and the ghetto might not be so wide as it now appears. I am at a loss to understand why Mr. Duberman excludes most of organized labor from the coalition but embraces "unskilled, ununionized laborers," unless he means to suggest that some political virtue resides among the unskilled and unorganized and that this virtue is contaminated by unionization. Here I fear Mr. Duberman may have succumbed to New Left romanticism. I am also skeptical of the progressive role he assigns to "new class technocrats," in whom I detect strong and dangerous currents of elitism. In glorifying this class, many New Leftists (I do not include Mr. Duberman) are disclosing more about their own class connections and semi-conscious ambitions than about the dynamics of social change. The proletariat having failed, history, they seem to say, has a new agent.

I doubt it.

BLACK POWER: RIGHT OR LEFT?

Julius W. Hobson

Writing from a Marxist perspective, Julius W. Hobson, chairman of the Washington, D.C. chapter of ACT, a civil rights organization, argues against Black Power's attempt to bring about changes within the present economic and political arrangements in the United States. He warns of the system's ability to obliterate or absorb its opponents.

At the Black Power Conference in Newark, New Jersey, I visited a half dozen committee meetings on subjects ranging from political theory to education, but perhaps the most important, and the most revealing, was the discussion by the committee on economics.

The general consensus of this gathering was that we needed to transfer the economic power wielded by white men in the Black ghettos of America to Black men. There were many proposals forthcoming on how this should be done. One minister proposed collecting a dollar from each Black man in the United States with which we would open up a bank. One self-styled revolutionary pointed out that the answer to the economic problems of Black people was the formation of cooperatives throughout the country, under Black control of course. There were lengthy papers prepared on the merits of Black ownership of ghetto housing, community control of service institutions and facilities, and even on the economic merits of a completely Black police force. Probably the most startling observation made in the economics committee meetings was the proposal that money be somehow kept in the Black community, and that that community become an economic entity or island on the larger American continent of capitalism.

The discussions within the political committee centered around the voting power of concentrated black enclaves within American cities. Somehow, it was pointed out, we could control our own destinies within the framework of the

From Floyd B. Barbour, ed., *The Black Power Revolt: A Collection of Essays* (Boston: Porter Sargeant Publisher, 1968), pp. 199–203. Reprinted by permission of Porter Sargeant Publisher. Copyright 1968 by Julius W. Hobson.

present political system, if we remained in the center cities and voted in blocks.

In still other committee meetings here were discussions and assurances on the subject of the beauty of blackness, and a reaffirmation of the obvious fact that men of color were handsome, and women of color were beautiful. So impressive were these discussions that one of the leading "revolutionaries" suggested in line with the disdain for all things white or light, that we change the English language to read "endarken" me instead of enlighten me.

The most obvious conclusions that could be drawn from all of this are (1) that the well-meaning proponents of these ideas were completely unaware of the degree to which they have already been "endarkened" by the good old American political and economic concepts of the status quo; and (2) that the agents of these ideas had little or no understanding of the nature of their political and economic surroundings; and (3) there was and still is a grave need to adopt a consistent philosophical base for the Black power movement.

The reality which the conference did not confront is this: that the history of social protest and change within the framework of capitalism everywhere, and at all times, has always been a history of the complete destruction or absorption of the agents of change.

The recent history of the American Labor Movement is an excellent case in point. . . . Another example of the futility of trying to make capitalism work, is the recent history of the late civil rights movement. From 1960 through 1964 the cry was integrate, Black and white together, and we shall overcome. The agents of these concepts (and I was taken too) spent immeasurable energy and time in freedom rides, sit-ins, live-ins, and marches, all designed to bring us into the promised land of the good old American economic system which we affectionately call capitalism.

Like the labor leaders of two decades earlier, civil rights leaders counseled their followers on the merits of gaining compatibility within the economic and political frameworks, and in a nonviolent fashion, no less. And in the mid 1960's as in the mid 1950's the skeptics either were dislodged from the "respectable" civil rights organizations and branded as militants, or recanted, and were invited to the White House as "responsible Negro leaders."

The Head of the Urban League, the "cleanest" civil rights organization, traveled to Vietnam and like the absorbed leaders of the past and present, endorsed the destruction of workers by workers, and all in the name of freedom, the free enterprise system, and Jesus Christ.

In my graduate student days my old and respected teacher of economic theory introduced his courses with the statement that "a capitalist is a capitalist regardless of race, creed or color." In his many enlightening lectures he proceeded to support this statement by pointing out that capitalism in all its history has been a system characterized by the unequal distribution of goods and services, by economic class structure, by exploitation, by profit motivation and by expansionism. The system has always found rationalizations for its behavior. My teacher defined racism as a rationalization for economic exploitation. It therefore followed, he said, that we cannot hope to eradicate racism from the United States and at the same time maintain capitalism. Private enterprisers have always and everywhere attempted to justify or rationalize their behavior, sometimes in the name of "progress," "civilization," Christianity, or as in Vietnam, in the name of world freedom and self-determination.

It was within the framework of the Socialist economics of Karl Marx that my teacher lectured. He pointed out what was indeed true, namely, that the Marxist doctrine was the most logical, most consistent and most obvious theoretical guide available to the oppressed who are seeking revolutionary change. The experiences in some Scandinavian countries give substance to the wisdom of my teacher's argument.

The logical conclusion drawn from all of this is that, given the same set of economic circumstances, a black slum lord will act exactly as the white slum lord acts. The black entrepreneur will be forced into perpetuating the system of exploitation if he operates as a capitalist. Black bankers will be dealing in the same money markets with their white counterparts and will thus be guided by the same rules of the banking game. In any system with primary property values, black policemen will protect black haves against the black have nots.

There is no evidence anywhere in the literature to support the idea that money can be kept within the geographical boundaries of any community. The characteristics of socialist as well as capitalist economic systems would not allow any such arrangement.

Any one familiar with the history of American cooperation, the farm cooperatives of the Mid-Western United States or the Rural electric cooperatives anywhere in the United States, is aware of the fact that cooperative efforts in this country have done little more than produce managerial classes with private enterprise mentalities.

Thus, we black power advocates face the decision either of duplicating the white man's mistakes by attempting to build an equally exploitative and racist black capitalism, or of internationalizing the struggle and moving with the tide of the oppressed peoples of the world toward an economic system based upon the socialist economics of Karl Marx.

If we adopt the latter, we will move in the direction of creating a world economy that produces for need rather than for profit. We will begin the creation of a system which has proven that it can eliminate starvation. We will foster the ownership of the world's natural re-

sources by the people of the world, and we will create economic circumstances in which men will cease the exploitation of other men for personal gain. And most important, we will be able to hail the beginnings of a selfless society in which property values will no longer supplant human values.

Black beauty indeed! I was glad to be kicked out of CORE in 1964 for running the Washington Chapter in an "undemocratic fashion" which facilitated Black control. Not that I thought Black control would bring about immediate revolution, but because I was sure then, and I am sure now, that if we are to have a revolution in America, Black men by virtue of their positions in this society must be the ones to lead it. I believed then, and I believe now, that the struggle for world freedom must move to the left toward socialism, and not to the right in any attempt to live with capitalism.

Black people in the United States are in dire need of the psychological freedom which the emphasis of blackness affords, but lest we forget, the struggle is multi-racial and worldwide. There are resources outside of our color-camp which we need and should utilize. There is a thin line between the concept of virtuous blackness and the concept of racism—the rightist doctrine for which we have justifiably condemned the white man. Let us learn from his history.

And so to the youthful black power advocates I would say, go left young men, for it will be a great day indeed when the world socialist camp prepares to receive this black division of the army of the proletariat which has been wandering in the American economic wilderness since 1865.

National Black Economic Development Conference

As publicly enunciated by James Forman, the Black Manifesto demanded $500 million in reparations to the black communities from the American churches. Its import is to be seen more in terms of the intensity of its rhetoric and its view that blacks are the potential liberators of American society, than for its programmatic contributions.

We the black people assembled in Detroit, Michigan for the National Black Economic Development Conference are fully aware that we have been forced to come together because racist white America has exploited our resources, our minds, our bodies, our labor. For centuries we have been forced to live as colonized people inside the United States, victimized by the most vicious, racist system in the world. We have helped to build the most industrial contry in the world.

We are therefore demanding of the white Christian churches and Jewish synagogues which are part and parcel of the system of capitalism, that they begin to pay reparations to black people in this country. We are demanding $500,000,000 from the Christian white churches and the Jewish synagogues. This total comes to 15 dollars per nigger. This is a low estimate for we maintain there are probably more than 30,000,000 black people in this country. $15 a nigger is not a large sum of money and we know that the churches and synagogues have a tremendous wealth and its membership, white America, has profited and still exploits black people. We are also not unaware that the exploitation of colored peoples around the world is aided and abetted by the white Christian churches and synagogues. This demand for $500,000,000 is not an idle resolution or empty words. Fifteen dollars for every black brother and sister in the United States is only a beginning of the reparations due us as people who have been exploited and degraded, bru-

talized, killed and persecuted. Underneath all of this exploitation, the racism of this country has produced a psychological effect upon us that we are beginning to shake off. We are no longer afraid to demand our full rights as a people in this decadent society.

We are demanding $500,000,000 to be spent in the following way:

1. We call for the establishment of a Southern land bank to help our brothers and sisters who have to leave their land because of racist pressure for people who want to establish cooperative farms, but who have no funds. We have seen too many farmers evicted from their homes because they have dared to defy the white racism of this country. We need money for land. We must fight for massive sums of money for this Southern Land Bank. We call for $200,000,000 to implement this program.

2. We call for the establishment of four major publishing and printing industries in the United States to be funded with ten million dollars each. These publishing houses are to be located in Detroit, Atlanta, Los Angeles, and New York. They will help to generate capital for further cooperative investments in the black community, provide jobs and an alternative to the white-dominated and controlled printing field.

3. We call for the establishment of four of the most advanced scientific and futuristic audio-visual networks to be located in Detroit, Chicago, Cleveland and Washington, D.C. These TV networks will provide an alternative to the

First enunciated at the Interreligious Foundation of Community Organizations, Inc., Detroit, April 1969.

racist propaganda that fills the current television networks. Each of these TV networks will be funded by ten million dollars each.

4. We call for a research skills center which will provide research on the problems of black people. This center must be funded with no less than 30 million dollars.

5. We call for the establishment of a training center for the teaching of skills in community organization, photography, movie making, television making and repair, radio building and repair and all other skills needed in communication. This training center shall be funded with no less than ten million dollars.

6. We recognize the role of the National Welfare Rights Organization and we intend to work with them. We call for ten million dollars to assist in the organization of welfare recipients. We want to organize the welfare workers in this country so that they may demand more money from the government and better administration of the welfare system of this country.

7. We call for $20,000,000 to establish a National Black Labor Strike and Defense Fund. This is necessary for the protection of black workers and their families who are fighting racist working conditions in this country.

*: We call for the establishment of the International Black Appeal (IBA). This International Black Appeal will be funded with no less than $20,000,000. The IBA is charged with producing more capital for the establishment of cooperative businesses in the United States and in Africa, our Motherland. The International Black Appeal is one of the most important demands that we are making for we know that it can generate and raise funds throughout the United States and help our African brothers. The IBA is charged with three functions and shall be headed by James Forman:

(a) Raising money for the program of the National Black Economic Development Conference.

* (Revised and approved by Steering Committee.)

(b) The development of cooperatives in African countries and support of African Liberation movements.

(c) Establishment of a Black Anti-Defamation League which will protect our African image.

9. We call for the establishment of a Black University to be funded with $130,000,000 to be located in the South. Negotiations are presently under way with a Southern University.

10. We demand that IFCO allocate all unused funds in the planning budget to implement the demands of this conference.

In order to win our demands we are aware that we will have to have massive support, therefore:

(1) We call upon all black people throughout the United States to consider themselves as members of the National Black Economic Development Conference and to act in unity to help force the racist white Christian churches and Jewish synagogues to implement these demands.

(2) We call upon all the concerned black people across the country to contact black workers, black women, black students and black unemployed, community groups, welfare organizations, teacher organizations, church leaders and organizations explaining how these demands are vital to the black community of the U.S. Pressure by whatever means necessary should be applied to the white power structure of the racist white Christian churches and Jewish synagogues. All black people should act boldly in confronting our white oppressors and demanding this modest reparation of 15 dollars per black man.

(3) Delegates and members of the National Black Economic Development Conference are urged to call press conferences in the cities and to attempt to get as many black organizations as possible to support the demands of the conference. The quick use of the press in the local areas will heighten the tension and these demands must be attempted to be won in a short period of time, although we are prepared for protracted and long range struggle.

(4) We call for the total disruption of selected church sponsored agencies operating anywhere in the U.S. and the world. Black workers, black women, black students and the black unemployed are encouraged to seize the offices, telephones, and printing apparatus of all church sponsored agencies and to hold these in trusteeship until our demands are met.

(5) We call upon all delegates and members of the National Black Economic Development Conference to stage sit-in demonstrations at selected black and white churches. This is not to be interpreted as a continuation of the sit-in movement of the early sixties but we know that active confrontation inside white churches is possible and will strengthen the possibility of meeting our demands. Such confrontation can take the form of reading the Black Manifesto instead of a sermon or passing it out to church members. The principle of self-defense should be applied if attacked.

(6) On May 4, 1969 or a date thereafter, depending upon local conditions, we call upon black people to commence the disruption of the racist churches and synagogues throughout the United States.

(7) We call upon IFCO to serve as a central staff to coordinate the mandate of the conference and to reproduce and distribute en mass literature, leaflets, news items, press releases and other material.

(8) We call upon all delegates to find within the white community those forces which will work under the leadership of blacks to implement these demands by whatever means necessary. By taking such actions, white Americans will demonstrate concretely that they are willing to fight the white skin privilege and the white supremacy and racism which has forced us as black people to make these demands.

(9) We call upon all white Christians and Jews to practice patience, tolerance, understanding, and nonviolence as they have encouraged, advised and demanded that we as black people should do throughout our entire enforced slavery in the United States. The true test of their faith and belief in the Cross and the words of the prophets will certainly be put to a test as we seek legitimate and extremely modest reparations for our role in developing the industrial base of the Western world through our slave labor. But we are no longer slaves, we are men and women, proud of our African heritage, determined to have our dignity.

(10) We are so proud of our African heritage and realize concretely that our struggle is not only to make revolution in the United States, but to protect our brothers and sisters in Africa and to help them rid themselves of racism, capitalism, and imperialism by whatever means necessary, including armed struggle. We are and must be willing to fight the defamation of our African image wherever it rears its ugly head. We are therefore charging the Steering Committee to create a Black Anti-Defamation League to be funded by money raised from the International Black appeal.

(11) We fully recognize that revolution in the United States and Africa, our Motherland, is more than a one dimensional operation. It will require the total integration of the political, economic, and military components and therefore, we call upon all our brothers and sisters who have acquired training and expertise in the fields of engineering, electronics, research, community organization, physics, biology, chemistry, mathematics, medicine, military science and warfare to assist the National Black Economic Development Conference in the implementation of its program.

(12) To implement these demands we must have a fearless leadership. We must have a leadership which is willing to battle the church establishment to implement these demands. To win our demands we will have to declare war on the white Christian churches and synagogues and this means we may have to fight the government structure of this country. Let no one here think that these demands will be met by our mere stating them. For the sake of the churches

and synagogues, we hope that they have the wisdom to understand that these demands are modest and reasonable. But if the white Christians and Jews are not willing to meet our demands through peace and good will, then we declare war and we are prepared to fight by whatever means necessary. . . .

Brothers and sisters, we no longer are shuffling our feet and scratching our heads. We are tall, black and proud.

And we say to the white Christian churches and Jewish synagogues, to the government of this country and to all the white racist imperialists who compose it, there is only one thing left that you can do to further degrade black people and that is to kill us. But we have been dying too long for this country. We have died in every war. We are dying in Vietnam today fighting the wrong enemy.

The new black man wants to live and to live means that we must not become static or merely believe in self-defense. We must boldly go out and attack the white Western world at its power centers. The white Christian churches are another form of government in this country and they are used by the government of this country to exploit the people of Latin America, Asia and Africa, but the day is soon coming to an end. Therefore, brothers and sisters, the demands we make upon the white Christian churches and the Jewish synagogues are small demands. They represent 15 dollars per black person in these United States. We can legitimately demand this from the church power structure. We must demand more from the United States Government.

But to win our demands from the church which is linked up with the United States Government, we must not forget that it will ultimately be by force and power that we will win.

We are not threatening the churches. We are saying that we know the churches came with the military might of the colonizers and have been sustained by the military might of the colonizers. Hence, if the churches in colonial territories were established by military might, we know deep within our

hearts that we must be prepared to us force to get our demands. We are no saying that this is the road we want t take. It is not, but let us be very clea that we are not opposed to force an we are not opposed to violence. We wer captured in Africa by violence. We wer kept in bondage and political servitud and forced to work as slaves by the mili tary machinery and the Christian churc working hand in hand.

We recognize that in issuing this man ifesto we must prepare for a long rang educational campaign in all communi ties of this country, but we know tha the Christian churches have contributed to our oppression in white America. We do not intend to abuse our black brothers and sisters in black churches who have uncritically accepted Christianity. We want them to understand how the rac ist white christian church with its hypo critical declarations and doctrines of brotherhood has abused our trust and faith. An attack on the religious beliefs of black people is not our major objec tive, even though we know that we were not Christians when we were brought to this country, but that Christianity was used to help enslave us. Our objec tive in issuing this Manifesto is to force the racist white Christian Church to be gin the payment of reparations which are due to all black people, not only by the church but also by private business and the U.S. government. We see this focus on the Christian Church as an ef fort around which all black people can unite.

Our demands are negotiable, but they cannot be minimized, they can only be increased and the Church is asked to. come up with larger sums of money than we are asking. Our slogans are:

ALL ROADS MUST LEAD TO REVOLUTION

UNITE WITH WHOMEVER YOU CAN UNITE

NEUTRALIZE WHEREVER POSSIBLE

FIGHT OUR ENEMIES RELENTLESSLY

VICTORY TO THE PEOPLE

LIFE AND GOOD HEALTH TO MANKIND

ESISTANCE TO DOMINATION BY THE WHITE
CHRISTIAN CHURCHES AND THE JEWISH
SYNAGOGUES

REVOLUTIONARY BLACK POWER

WE SHALL WIN WITHOUT A DOUBT

ECIPROCAL BASES OF NATIONAL CULTURE AND THE FIGHT FOR FREEDOM

rantz Fanon

*rantz Fanon was one of the first black theorists (Martinique) to ex-
ound upon the theme of black consciousness as a first step towards
lack liberation. Although African, his influence on a section of the black
ower movement, in particular on young black students, has been
narked. At the time of this writing Fanon was a practicing psychiatrist
n Algeria.*

The nation is not only the condition of culture, its fruitfulness, its continuous renewal, and its deepening. It is also a necessity. It is the fight for national existence which sets culture moving and opens to it the doors of creation. Later on it is the nation which will ensure the conditions and framework necessary to culture. The nation gathers together the various indispensable elements necessary for the creation of a culture, those elements which alone can give it credibility, validity, life and creative power. In the same way it is its national character that will make such a culture open to other cultures and which will enable it to influence and permeate other cultures. A non-existent culture can hardly be expected to have bearing on reality, or to influence reality. The first necessity is the re-establishment of the nation in order to give life to national culture in the strictly biological sense of the phrase.

Thus we have followed the break-up of the old strata of culture, a shattering which becomes increasingly fundamental; and we have noticed, on the eve of the decisive conflict for national freedom, the renewing of forms of expression and the rebirth of the imagination. There remains one essential question:

what are the relations between the struggle—whether political or military—and culture? Is there a suspension of culture during the conflict? Is the national struggle an expression of a culture? Finally, ought one to say that the battle for freedom however fertile *a posteriori* with regard to culture is in itself a negation of culture? In short, is the struggle for liberation a cultural phenomenon or not?

We believe that the conscious and organised undertaking by a colonised people to re-establish the sovereignty of that nation constitutes the most complete and obvious cultural manifestation that exists. It is not alone the success of the struggle which afterwards gives validity and vigour to culture; culture is not put into cold storage during the conflict. The struggle itself in its development and in its internal progression sends culture along different paths and traces out entirely new ones for it. The struggle for freedom does not give back to the national culture its former value and shapes; this struggle which aims at a fundamentally different set of relations between men cannot leave intact either the form or the content of the people's culture. After the conflict there is not only the disappearance of colonialism

From *The Wretched of the Earth* (New York: Grove Press, 1963), pp. 196–199. Copyright 1963 by Presence Africaine. Reprinted by permission of Grove Press, Inc.

but also the disappearance of the colonised man.

This new humanity cannot do otherwise than define a new humanism both for itself and for others. It is prefigured in the objectives and methods of the conflict. A struggle which mobilises all classes of the people and which expresses their aims and their impatience, which is not afraid to count almost exclusively on the people's support, will of necessity triumph. The value of this type of conflict is that it supplies the maximum of conditions necessary for the development and aims of culture. After national freedom has been obtained in these conditions, there is no such painful cultural indecision which is found in certain countries which are newly independent, because the nation by its manner of coming into being and in the terms of its existence exerts a fundamental influence over culture. A nation which is born of the people's concerted action and which embodies the real aspirations of the people while changing the State cannot exist save in the expression of exceptionally rich forms of culture.

The natives who are anxious for the culture of their country and who wish to give to it a universal dimension ought not therefore to place their confidence in the single principle of inevitable, undifferentiated independence written into the consciousness of the people in order to achieve their task. The liberation of the nation is one thing; the methods and popular content of the fight are another. It seems to us that the future of national culture and its riches are equally also part and parcel of the values which have ordained the struggle for freedom.

And now it is time to denounce certain pharisees. National claims, it is here and there stated, are a phase that humanity has left behind. It is the day of great concerted actions, and retarded nationalists ought in consequence to set their mistakes aright. We however consider that the mistake, which may have very serious consequences, lies in wishing to skip the national period. If culture is the expression of national consciousness, I will not hesitate to affirm that in the case with which we are dealing it is the national consciousness which is the most elaborate form of culture.

The consciousness of self is not the closing of a door to communication. Philosophic thought teaches us, on the contrary, that it is its guarantee. National consciousness, which is not nationalism, is the only thing that will give us an international dimension. This problem of national consciousness and of national culture takes on in Africa a special dimension. The birth of national consciousness in Africa has a strictly contemporaneous connection with the African consciousness. The responsibility of the African as regards national culture is also a responsibility with regard to African Negro culture. This joint responsibility is not the fact of a metaphysical principle but the awareness of a simple rule which wills that every independent nation in an Africa where colonialism is still entrenched is an encircled nation, a nation which is fragile and in permanent danger.

If man is known by his acts, then we will say that the most urgent thing today for the intellectual is to build up his nation. If this building up is true, that is to say if it interprets the manifest will of the people and reveals the eager African peoples, then the building of a nation is of necessity accompanied by the discovery and encouragement of universaling values. Far from keeping aloof from other nations, therefore, it is national liberation which leads the nation to play its part on the stage of history. It is at the heart of national consciousness that international consciousness lives and grows. And this two-fold emerging is ultimately only the source of all culture.

Statement made at the Second Congress of Black Artists and Writers, Rome, 1959.

CONVALESCENCE

Eldridge Cleaver

Almost all discussions of Black Power fail to raise certain psychosexual questions about the nature of blackness and white perceptions of black sexuality. And yet, Gunnar Myrdal emphasizes the importance of these perceptions in his classic study on the Negro. In this post-Freudian age, the omission of this discussion in current literature is all the more surprising. Eldridge Cleaver, Minister of Information for the Black Panther Party, symbolically raises the issue of Negritude and black personality in the following selection by pitting a white Omnipotent Administrator against a black Supermasculine Menial. In the tradition of Norman Mailer and James Baldwin, Cleaver asks that we face up to the black/white confrontation and its roots in man's sexual instincts and cultural accommodations. In political terms, the argument would have to be made that if there is a "black essence" —call it Negritude or soul—then one can make a strong case for rejecting coalition politics.

If the separation of the black and white people in America along the color line had the effect, in terms of social imagery, of separating the Mind from the Body—the oppressor whites usurping sovereignty by monopolizing the Mind, abdicating the Body and becoming bodiless Omnipotent Administrators and Ultrafemines; and the oppressed blacks, divested of sovereignty and therefore of Mind, manifesting the Body and becoming mindless Supermasculine Menials and Black Amazons—if this is so, then the 1954 U.S. Supreme Court decision in the case of *Brown* v. *Board of Education,* demolishing the principle of segregation of the races in public education and striking at the very root of the practice of segregation generally, was a major surgical operation performed by nine men in black robes on the racial Maginot Line which is imbedded as deep as sex or the lust for lucre in the schismatic American psyche. This piece of social surgery, if successful, performed without benefit of any anesthetic except God and the Constitution, in a land where God is dead and the Constitution has been in a coma for 180 years, is more marvelous than a successful heart transplant would be, for it was meant to graft the nation's Mind back onto its Body and vice versa.

If the foregoing is true, then the history of America in the years following the pivotal Supreme Court edict should be a record of the convalescence of the nation. And upon investigation we should be able to see the Omnipotent Administrators and Ultrafemines grappling with their unfamiliar and alienated Bodies, and the Supermasculine Menials and Amazons attempting to acquire and assert *a mind of their own.* The record, I think, is clear and unequivocal. The bargain which seems to have been struck is that the whites have had to turn to the blacks for a clue on how to swing with the Body, while the blacks have had to turn to the whites for the secret of the Mind. It was Chubby Checker's mission, bearing the Twist as *good news,* to teach the whites, whom history had taught to forget, how to shake their asses again. It is a skill they surely must once have possessed but which they abandoned for puritanical dreams of escaping the corruption of the flesh, by leaving the terrors of the Body to the blacks.

In the swift, fierce years since the 1954 school desegregation decision, a rash of seemingly unrelated mass phenomena has appeared on the American scene—deviating radically from the prevailing Hot-Dog-and-Malted-Milk norm of the bloodless, square, superficial, faceless Sunday-Morning atmosphere that was suffocating the nation's soul. And all of this in a nation where the so-called molders of public opinion, the writers, politicians, teachers, and cab drivers, are willful, euphoric liars or zip-dam ostriches and owls, a clique of undercover ghosts, a bunch of Walter Jenkinses, a lot of coffee-drinking, cigarette-smoking, sly, suck-assing, status-seeking cheating, nervous, dry-balled, tranquilizer-gulched, countdown-minded, out-of-style, slithering snakes. No wonder that many "innocent people," the manipulated and the stimulated, some of whom were game for a reasonable amount of mystery and even adventure, had their minds scrambled. These observers were not equipped to either *feel* or *know* that a radical break, a revolutionary leap out of their sight, had taken place in the secret parts of this nation's soul. It was as if a driverless vehicle were speeding through the American night down an unlighted street toward a stone wall and was boarded on the fly by a stealthy ghost with a drooling leer on his face, who, at the last detour before chaos and disaster, careened the vehicle down a smooth highway that leads to the future and life; and to ask these Americans to understand that they were the passengers on this driverless vehicle and that the lascivious ghost was the Saturday-night crotchfunk of the Twist, or the "Yeah, Yeah, Yeah!" which the Beatles highjacked from Ray Charles, to ask these Calvinistic profligates to see the logical and reciprocal links is more cruel than asking a hope-to-die Okie Music buff to cop the sounds of John Coltrane.

In the beginning of the era came a thief with a seven-year itch who knew that the ostriches and the owls had been bribed with a fix of Euphony, which is their kick. The thief knew that he need not wait for the cover of night, that with impunity he could show his face in the marketplace in the full light of the sun, do his deed, scratch his dirt, sell his loot to the fence while the ostriches and owls, coasting on Euphony, one with his head in a hole—any hole—and the other with his head in the clouds, would only cluck and whisper and hear-see-speak no evil.

So Elvis Presley came, strumming a weird guitar and wagging his tail across the continent, ripping off fame and fortune as he scrunched his way, and, like a latter-day Johnny Appleseed, sowing seeds of a new rhythm and style in the white souls of the white youth of America, whose inner hunger and need was no longer satisfied with the antiseptic white shoes and whiter songs of Pat Boone. "You can do anything," sang Elvis to Pat Boone's white shoes, "but don't you step on my Blue Suede Shoes!"

During this period of ferment and beginnings, at about the same time that the blacks of Montgomery, Alabama, began their historic bus boycott (giving birth to the leadership of Martin Luther King, signifying to the nation that, with this initiative, this first affirmative step, somewhere in the universe a gear in the machinery had shifted), something, a target, came into focus. The tensions in the American psyche had torn a fissure in the racial Maginot Line and through this fissure, this tiny bridge between the Mind and Body, the black masses, who had been silent and somnolent since the '20s and '30s, were now making a break toward the dimly seen light that beckoned to them through the fissure. The fact that these blacks could now take such a step was perceived by the ostriches and owls as a sign of national decay, a sign that the System had caved in at that spot. And this gave birth to a fear, a fear that quickly became a focus for all the anxieties and exasperations in the Omnipotent Administrators' minds; and to embody this perceived decay and act as a lightning rod for the fear, the beatniks bloomed onto the American scene.

Like pioneers staking their claims in the no-man's land that lay along the racial Maginot Line, the beatniks, like Elvis Presley before them, dared to do in the light of day what America had long been doing in the sneak-thief anonymity of night—consorted on a human level with the blacks. Reviled, cursed, held in contempt by the "molders of public opinion," persecuted by the police, made into an epithet of derision by the deep-frozen geeks of the Hot-Dog-and-Malted-Milk set, the beatniks irreverently refused to go away. Allen Ginsberg and Jack Kerouac ("the Suzuki rhythm boys," James Baldwin called them, derisively, in a moment of panic, "tired of white ambitions" and "dragging themselves through the Negro street at dawn, looking for an angry fix"; "with," as Mailer put it, "the black man's code to fit their facts"). Bing Crosbyism, Perry Comoism, and Dinah Shoreism had led to cancer, and the vanguard of the white youth knew it.

And as the spirit of revolt crept across the continent from that wayward bus in Montgomery, Albama, seeping like new life into the cracks and nooks of the northern ghettos and sweeping in furious gales across the campuses of southern Negro colleges, erupting, finally, in the sit-ins and freedom rides—as this swirling maelstrom of social change convulsed the nation, shocking an unsuspecting American public, folk music, speaking of fundamental verities, climbed slowly out of the grave; and the hip lobe of the national ear, twitching involuntarily at first, began to listen.

From the moment that Mrs. Rosa Parks, in that bus in Montgomery, Alabama, resisted the Omnipotent Administrator, contact, however fleeting, had been made with the lost sovereignty— the Body had made contact with its Mind —and the shock of that contact sent an electric current throughout this nation, traversing the racial Maginot Line and striking fire in the hearts of the whites. The wheels began to turn, the thaw set in, and though Emmett Till and Mack Parker were dead, though Eisenhower sent troops to Little Rock, though Autherine Lucy's token presence at the University of Alabama was a mockery —notwithstanding this, it was already clear that the 1954 major surgical operation had been successful and the patient would live. The challenge loomed on the horizon: Africa, black, enigmatic, and hard-driving, had begun to parade its newly freed nations into the UN; and the Islam of Elijah Muhammad, amplified as it was fired in salvos from the piercing tongue of Malcolm X, was racing through the Negro streets with Allen Ginsberg and Jack Kerouac.

Then, as the verbal revolt of the black masses soared to a cacophonous peak —the Body, the Black Amazons and Supermasculine Menials, becoming conscious, shouting, in a thousand different ways, *I've got a Mind of my own!*"; and as the senator from Massachusetts was saving the nation from the Strangelove grasp of Dirty Dick, injecting, as he emerged victorious, a new and vivacious spirit into the people with the style of his smile and his wife's hairdo; then, as if a signal had been given, as if the Mind had shouted to the Body, "I'm ready!"—the Twist, superseding the Hula Hoop, burst upon the scene like a nuclear explosion, sending its fallout of rhythm into the Minds and Bodies of the people. The fallout: the Hully Gully, the Mashed Potato, the Dog, the Smashed Banana, the Watusi, the Frug, the Swim. The Twist was a guided missile, launched from the ghetto into the very heart of suburbia. The Twist succeeded, as politics, religion, and law could never do, in writing in the heart and soul what the Supreme Court could only write on the books. The Twist was a form of therapy for a convalescing nation. The Omnipotent Administrator and the Ultrafeminine responded so dramatically in stampede fashion, to the Twist precisely because it afforded them the possibility of reclaiming their Bodies again after generations of alienated and disembodied existence.

The stiff, mechanical Omnipotent Administrators and Ultrafeminines presented a startling spectacle as they entered in droves onto the dance floors to learn how to Twist. They came from every level of society, from top to bottom, writhing pitifully though gamely about the floor, feeling exhilarating and soothing new sensations, release from some unknown prison in which their Bodies had been encased, a sense of freedom they had never known before, a feeling of communion with some mystical root-source of life and vigor, from which sprang a new awareness and enjoyment of the flesh, a new appreciation of the possibilities of their Bodies. They were swinging and gyrating and shaking their dead little asses like petrified zombies trying to regain the warmth of life, re-kindle the dead limbs, the cold ass, the stone heart, the stiff, mechanical, dis-used joints with the spark of life.

This spectacle truly startled many Negroes, because they perceived it as an intrusion by the Mind into the province of the Body, and this intimated chaos; because the Negroes knew, from the survival experience of their everyday lives, that the system within which they were imprisoned was based upon the racial Maginot Line and that the cardinal sin, crossing the line—which was, in their experience, usually initiated from the black side—was being committed, *en masse*, by the whites. The Omnipotent Administrators and Ultrafeminines were storming the Maginot Line! A massive assault had been launched without parallel in American history, and to Negroes it was confusing. Sure, they had witnessed it on an individual scale: they had seen many ofays destroy the Maginot Line in themselves. But this time it had all the appearances of a national movement. There were even rumors that President Kennedy and his Jackie were doing the Twist secretly in the White House; that their Number One Boy had been sent to the Peppermint Lounge in disguise to learn how to Twist, and he in turn brought the trick back to the White House. These Negroes knew that something fundamental had changed.

"Man, what done got into them ofays?" one asked.

"They trying to get back," said another.

"Shit," said a young Negro who made his living by shoplifting. "If you ask me, I think it must be the end of the world."

"Oooo-weee!" said a Negro musician who had been playing at a dance and was now standing back checking the dancers. "Baby, I don't dig this action at all! Look here, baby, pull my coat to what's going down! I mean, have I missed it somewhere? Where've I been? Baby, I been blowing all my life and I ain't never dug no happenings like this. You know what, man, I'm gon' cut that fucking weed aloose. Oooo-weee! Check that little bitch right there! What the fuck she trying to do? Is she trying to shake it or break it? Oooo-weee!"

A Negro girl said: "Take me home, I'm sick!"

Another one said: "No, let's stay! This is too much!"

And a bearded Negro cat, who was not interested in learning how to Twist himself, who felt that if he was interested in doing it, he could get up from the table right now and start Twisting, he said, sitting at the table with a tinsel-minded female: "It ain't nothing. They just trying to get back, that's all."

"Get back?" said the girl, arching her brows quizzically, "Get back from where?"

"From wherever they've been," said the cat, "where else?"

"Are they doing it in Mississippi is what I want to know," said a tall, deadly looking Negro who had a long razor line down his left cheek and who had left Mississippi in a hurry one night.

And the dancers: they were caught up in a whirl of ecstasy, swinging like pendulums, mechanical like metronomes or puppets on invisible strings being manipulated by a master with a sick sense of humor. "They look like Chinese doing communal exercise," said a Negro. "That's all they're doing, calisthenics!"

"Yeah, said his companion. "They're trying to get in shape."

But if at first it was funny and confusing, it was nonetheless a breakthrough. The Omnipotent Administrators and Ultrafeminines were discovering new aspects of the Body, new possibilities of rhythm, new ways to move. The Hula Hoop had been a false start, a mechanized, theatrical attempt by the Mind to supply to itself what only the Body can give. But, with the Twist, at last they knew themselves to be swinging. The forces acting upon the world stage in our era had created, in the collective psyche of the Omnipotent Administrators and Ultrafeminines, an irresistible urge —to just stand up and shake the ice and cancer out of their alienated white asses—and the Hula Hoop and Twist offered socially acceptable ways to do it.

Of course, not all the whites took part in these joyful experiments. For many, the more "suggestive" a dance became —i.e., the more it became pure Body and less Mind—the more scandalous it seemed to them; and their reaction in this sense was an index to the degree of their alienation from their Bodies. But what they condemned as a sign of degeneracy and moral decay was actually a sign of health, a sign of hope for full recovery. As Norman Mailer prophesied: ". . . the Negro's equality would tear a profound shift into the psychology, the sexuality, and the moral imagination of every white alive." Precisely because the Mind will have united with the Body, theory will have merged with practice.

It is significant that the Twist and the Hula Hoop came into the scene in all their fury at the close of the Eisenhower and the dawn of the Kennedy era. It could be interpreted as a rebellion against the vacuous Eisenhower years. It could also be argued that the same collective urge that gave rise to the Twist also swept Kennedy into office. I shudder to think that, given the closeness of the final vote in 1960, Richard Nixon might have won the election in a breeze if he had persuaded one of his Ultrafeminine daughters, not to mention Ultrapat, to do the Twist in public. Not if Kennedy had stayed on the phone a week sympathizing with Mrs. Martin Luther King, Jr., over the fact that the cat was in jail, would he have won. Even as I am convinced that Luci Baines Johnson, dancing the Watusi in public with Killer Joe Piro, won more votes for her old man in 1964 than a whole boxcar full of his hog-calling speeches ever did.

When the Birmingham Revolt erupted in the summer of 1963 and President Kennedy stepped into the void and delivered his unprecedented speech to the nation on civil rights and sent his bill to Congress, the foundation had been completed. Martin Luther King, Jr., giving voice to the needs of the Body, and President Kennedy, speaking out the needs of the Mind, made contact on that day. The Twisters, sporting their blue suede shoes, moved beyond the ghost in white shoes who ate a Hot Dog and sipped Malted Milk as he danced the mechanical jig of Satan on top of Medgar Evers' tomb. In vain now would the murderers bomb that church and slaughter grotesquely those four little black girls (what did they hope to kill? were they striking at the black of the skin or the fire of the soul? at history? at the Body?). In vain also the assassins' bullets that crashed through the head of John Kennedy, taking a life, yes, but creating a larger-than-life and failing utterly to expunge from the record the March on Washington and its truth: that this nation—bourgeois or not, imperialist or not, murderous or not, ugly or not—its people, somewhere in their butchered and hypocritical souls, still contained an epic potential of spirit which is its hope, a bottomless potential which fires the imaginations of its youth. It was all too late. It was too late because it was time for the blacks ("I've got a *Mind* of my own!") to riot, to sweep through the Harlem night like a wave of locusts, breaking, screaming, bleeding, laughing, crying, rejoicing, celebrating, in a jubilee of destruction, to regurgitate the white man's bullshit they'd been eating for four hundred years; smashing the windows of the white man's stores, throwing bricks they wished were bombs running, leaping whirling like a cyclone through the white man's Mind, past his backlash, through the night streets of Rochester, New Jersey, Philadelphia. And even though the opposition, gorging on Hot Dogs and Malted Milk, with blood now splattered over the white shoes, would still strike out in the dark against the manifestations of the turning, showing the protocol of Southern Hospitality reserved for Niggers and Nigger Lovers—*SCHWERNER-CHANEY-GOODMAN*—it was still too late. For not only had Luci Baines Johnson danced the Watusi in public with Killer Joe, but the Beatles were on the scene, injecting Negritude by the ton into the whites, in this post-Elvis Presley-beatnik era of ferment.

Before we toss the Beatles a homosexual kiss—saying, "If a man be ass enough to reach for the bitch in them, that man will kiss a man, and if a woman reaches for the stud in them, that woman will kiss a woman"—let us marvel at the genius of their image, which comforts the owls and ostriches in the one spot where Elvis Presley bummed their kick: Elvis, with his *un*-funky (yet mechanical, alienated) bumpgrinding, was still too much Body (too soon) for the strained collapsing psyches of the Omnipotent Administrators and Ultrafeminines; whereas the Beatles, affecting the caucasoid crown of femininity and ignoring the Body on the visual plane (while their music on the contrary being full of Body), assuaged the doubts of the owls and ostriches by presenting an incorporeal, cerebral image.

Song and dance are, perhaps, only a little less old than man himself. It is with his music and dance, the recreation through art of the rhythms suggested by and implicit in the tempo of his life and cultural environment, that man purges his soul of the tensions of daily strife and maintains his harmony in the universe. In the increasingly mechanized, automated, cybernated environment of the modern world—a cold, bodiless world of wheels, smooth plastic surfaces, tubes, pushbuttons, transistors, computers, jet propulsion, rockets to the moon, atomic energy—man's need for affirmation of his biology has become that much more intense. He feels need for a clear definition of where his body ends and the machine begins, where man ends and the *extensions* of man begin. This great mass hunger, which transcends national or racial boundaries, recoils from the subtle subversions of the mechanical environment which modern technology is creating faster than man, with his present savage relationship to his fellow men, is able to receive and assimilate. This is the central contradiction of the twentieth century; and it is against this backdrop

that America's attempt to unite its Mind with its Body, to save its soul, is taking place.

It is in this connection that the blacks, personifying the Body and thereby in closer communion with their biological roots than other Americans, provide the saving link, the bridge between man's biology and man's machines. In its purest form, as adjustment to the scientific and technological environment of our era, as purgative and lullaby-soother of man's soul, it is the jazz issuing from the friction and harmony of the American Negro with his environment that captured the beat and tempo of our times. And although modern science and technology are the same whether in New York, Paris, London, Accra, Cairo, Berlin, Moscow, Tokyo, Peking, or São Paulo, jazz is the only true international medium of communication current in the world today, capable of speaking creatively, with equal intensity and relevance, to the people in all those places.

The less sophisticated (but no less Body-based) popular music of urban Negroes—which was known as Rhythm and Blues before the whites appropriated and distilled it into a product they called Rock 'n Roll—is the basic ingredient, the core, of the gaudy, cacophonous hymns with which the Beatles of Liverpool drive their hordes of Ultrafeminine fans into catatonia and hysteria. For Beatle fans, having been alienated from their own Bodies so long and so deeply, the effect of these potent, erotic rhythms is electric. Into this music, the Negro projected—as it were, *drained off*, as pus from a sore—a powerful sensuality, his pain and lust, his love and his hate, his ambition and his despair. The Negro projected into his music his very Body. The Beatles, the four long-haired lads from Liverpool, are offering up as their gift the Negro's Body, and in so doing establish a rhythmic communication between the listener's own Mind and Body.

Enter the Beatles—soul by proxy, middlemen between the Mind and the Body. A long way from Pat Boone's White Shoes. A way station on a slow route traveled with all deliberate speed.

4 The Revolt And Social Change

EPILOGUE: THE PHENOMENON OF GHETTO LIFE

Sondra Silverman

Riots have marked the political scene since 1964, and there is little indication that they are simply a passing phase. In this selection, Sondra Silverman, who teaches political science in New York City, analyzes riots as a form of collective political behavior—a logical extension and a functional component of ghetto life. She argues that only by viewing the white world through the eyes of black America will we be able to understand the tensions underlying the integration-separatist debate among the blacks and the crisis with which the pluralist corporate state is confronted.

In analyzing the situation within the black ghettos, two sets of questions are raised: one on the thought processes of the concrete social actors, and the other on the observed consequences of the actors' actions. The analyst must describe and record the overt behavior of black social actors and imagine himself into the psychic and social world of the black ghetto. Once having understood the social act, the analyst then engages himself in its development. And in so far as he sees what it means—what it appears to be now and what it has the potential to develop into—he can evaluate its progression. For the phenomena of ghetto life are types of social action or social acts which may involve one set of ideas to its participants and another set to its observers. The social and political world of the ghetto resident is taken for granted by him; but to the others outside his life-turf, reality is of a different perceptual content. What is

right, proper and dignified for the outsiders is not necessarily a standard shared by those within the ghetto. What is expected behavior inside the ghetto may be condemned behavior outside it. The assumptions, the choices, and the solutions to life's daily routine may differ as soon as one reaches the north corner of 125th Street, New York.

This being the case, the argument here is that the meaning which ghetto life has for ghetto blacks needs to be understood on its own terms. Only in this way will the outsider, the interpreter, begin to understand an alien culture where what is believed and what is considered relevant is structured and accepted. A riot mirrors ghetto life, pointing up, dramatically and instantly, the life scene of the majority of America's blacks. Riots, as microcosms of ghetto life, mirror the frustrations and despair which are no longer capable of being contained inwardly, against the self, or

This article was written especially for this reader.

outwardly, against a single indentifiable object. Rather, riots are statements of anger expressing the relationships between the rioter and his immediate and distant worlds. They are unequivocal, hide nothing, obfuscate and confuse little, and reveal much in an action language few can avoid hearing even if many can misunderstand and misinterpret. They are manifestations of life in the subculture of a subject people—a way of achieving self in the larger society and a way of defining self according to the cognitive map of that society. But at the same time, a riot is a threat, a threat to the stability of the social order, to those who own the goods of the social order, to those who orient their behavior about a set of expectations based on the present order and set of conditions. It is a confrontation, and as in any confrontation, someone, usually he who has the superior armed strength, is going to come out the winner. A riot is a political act, a form of conflict between the perceived interests of the blacks and the perceived interests of the white community; it is an integral part of the power game.

A riot is complex not in terms of its performance but because of the duality mentioned before—the different meanings it has for the rioter and the observer, onlooker, political authority or social critic. However much we may quantify the phenomena, however much we may try to measure it on any given continuum of political action, we are still left with a subjective and an objective meaning in the precise sense in which those terms are used. Despite their differences, both meanings have truth value in that both are verifiable on their own terms. As analysts, we are concerned with the inter-relationships of these two meanings and the implications of their dichotomized perceptions: How different are the world views inside and outside the ghetto? What, if any, are the coincident value structures and ethical beliefs, group norms and social roles, which those who are black and those who are white have? What behavior patterns are shared by those who are defined, or who define them-

selves on the basis of skin pigmentation? Are all Negroes placed in such a common position in the social system that they develop a set of characteristics that allow them and others to think of them in group terms? These are some of the questions related to the reality of ghetto world raised by a study of riots.

I

By 1964, the civil rights movement had several minor successes to its credit: a piece of legislation, the Civil Rights Act of 1964, which helped to detroy the legal foundations of racisim but which ignored the problems facing the mass of ghetto blacks; the furthering of efforts, both organizational and psychological, to solidify the Negro race; the initiation within sections of the white community, especially among younger members of the New Left, of debates about the purposes to which the American economy and American political resources were being put to use. But these were insufficient to syphon off growing black discontent. If anything, having tasted the fruits of minor victory, appetites were whetted for improved conditions; and it now took even less, in incidental terms, to make Negroes feel more frustrated and discouraged with the American scene. The civil rights movement had lowered the threshold for rebellion; and while there had been some meaningful accomplishments for those middleclass and professional Negroes who comprised (only a small percentage of the race), the message of the need for more radical social change had not been confined to those few.

Within the framework of an integration strategy—for until this time Negro demands had been for the right to share in the advantages and privileges whites possessed, to be brought into the white house, burning (as Baldwin would put it) or not—there was a multitude of direct action tactics. Court litigation, lobbying, picketing, boycotts, voter registration and voter education drives, marches, freedom rides, sit-ins, stall-ins, chain-ins, kneel-ins—these and other forms of activity were methods of raising those demands that Negroes wanted to be heard and answered. But parallel to these tactics in the civil rights movement was a more intense and volatile method: violence. Riots broke out in urban centers of the United States—in ghetto areas where blacks lived in crowded, tense conditions, alienated from the socio-cultural world of white America and apathetic towards the political processes which governed the white mainstream. The ghettos were powder kegs, ready to explode at any time, should a match be dropped and a minor incident escalated into a major, violent outburst. A white policeman kills a black youth whom he suspects of being drunk and of having committed a robbery, or closes down a Negro club which he believes to be a brothel, or tows away an old car which he thinks is either stolen or abandoned by a resident of the black ghetto. Instantly, certain things become apparent to the crowd that gathers at the scene of the incident: "whitey" or "honkie," here in the form of the policeman, who has been blamed for deprivations and acts of violence in the past, becomes the enemy— the symbol of accumulated white-black antagonisms. With temper at heat, and usually temperatures the same, the ghetto dwellers do not decide to lodge a peaceful complaint against the policeman, for this is seen as an inadequate, ineffectual response. It is believed that rioters, assuming this role as in a play, performing it for a short time, and then resuming their more ordinary way of daily accommodation, will even the score. They will express their pent-up resentment by their physical release; they will get their revenge on "whitey" in their own retributive way, by attacking the sanctity of white property and getting some of the white goods as a reward to boot.

In the intensity of the ghetto, with its norms of violence and crime (a subculture of violence in a culture of violence), the explosion is easily set off. Mob action begins. Law and order, at the best of times tangential to the community, break down. Ill-assorted weapons are thrown at the police. Molotov cocktails explode. Sniper fire shatters the atmosphere. Fires start. Store windows are broken. Looting begins. Cars are overturned. There is an admixture of blood, cries, pain, laughs—the destruction of a Vietnamese village occasionally crossed with the carnival excitement of a Mardi Gras, but both are to the tunes of roaring sirens and neither to the sensuality of a black blues beat. No one is safe in the riot locale, although whites who chance to be there and white property which is entrenched all around are up for first grab. Blood brothers may be injured, but more often by accident than by design. There is no ghetto leadership either able or willing to calm the crowds who boo, spit, and attack those who try to use the reason and restraint alien to the situation. Only the outside political authorities with their superior forces—their tanks, armored cars, tear gas, mace, pistolry— can restore order, slowly and at a price in lives and property above that taken by the hatred and confusion of the rioters themselves. Even in Cleveland, where when the riots broke out in the summer of 1968 there was a Negro mayor in office, the state national guard had to win the armed confrontation before the peacemakers of the black community could go in and discuss the costs to be borne by the ghetto dwellers should the conflict be prolonged or started anew. For no matter how strategically placed the ghetto sniper may be, when he is confronted with authorities that are prepared to wipe him out at any price, he can no longer play for the prize of destroying his opponent. The cost of killing the enemy becomes a strategic question, and how much internal damage a tactical consideration.

The outstanding characteristic of the riots of the 1960's, distinguishing them from earlier race riots in American history, is that these were not the actions of white mobs against black mobs pitched in battle on the periphery of a black-white community. The recent riots were incidents of scattered Negro groups violently exploding in the ghetto against symbols of white perpetuation of racism. They involved attacks on the holdings of the white power structure, be that a white policeman, a pawnshop owned by a white businessman, or a delapidated rooming house owned by a white slumlord. Damages were confined to the ghetto, to the blacks who lived there, and to the whites who lived off of these blacks. Only infrequently—at least to the point of this writing—was there an occasional excursion into the white business district to loot a jewelry or a clothing store.

But even this internal damage was more than simply self-destruction, more than a series of melees with little or no direction, more than "senseless attacks on all constituted authority without purpose or object,"[1] as the Federal Bureau of Investigation suggested when the riots first began. Riots, for the rioters, were more than the rantings of an oppressed people, "full of sound and fury, signifying nothing." They were aggressive, political acts of the debtors against the creditors, or against the protectors (the police) of the creditors. They were attacks on the economic exploiters of the ghetto, men who live in the ghetto by day, and have the means to escape to white affluence at night. Riots are political responses in a form necessary for a leaderless people; they are uprisings of a disorganized community. To discuss them as less is to fail to perceive the social world of the ghetto and the political pictures the rioters perceive. Rioters are, in some ways, similar to Hobsbawm's "primitive rebels,"[2] but their action is "pre-political" only if we narrowly defined political in terms of an *institutionalized* struggle for power. Rioters are necessarily consequential when seen as facing the problem of adaptation to an industrial order which has treated them in what they consider to be a discriminatory, unjust, unfair way. They respond with vengeance, disrupting the political processes from which they have been excluded.

Who are the rioters? The rioters are the ghetto people. A more precise answer, based on analyses of arrest records and participant observation, seems to suggest that different and diverse groups contribute their efforts to the riot: teenagers and young men, many of whom are on school vacation or unemployed; housewives taking their share of luxury items from stores which have been broken into; technical workers, teachers, elevator operators caught up in the spirit of the occasion and made militant by the moment; armed black insurrectionaries, for whom the riot becomes another plank in a political program. These do not belong to the lowest class or are not fringe groups of criminal types. Rather, they are what Clark calls "marginal Negroes who were upwardly mobile—demanding a higher status than their families had."[3]

Profiles of rioters in Watts and Detroit support Clark's analysis that a predominant type of rioter was the aspiring young adult, employed and with some education[4]—again the Tocqueville thesis of rising expectations. And in the *Report of the National Advisory Commission on Civil Disorders*, there is a similar profile of rioters, although here there is emphasis on those who are occasionally unemployed or have jobs as unskilled or semi-skilled workers and who, in terms of stratification, are of low status. In addition, the *Report* continues: "He takes great pride in his race and believes that in some respects Negroes are superior to whites. . . . He is substantially better in-

[1] "Text of F.B.I. Report to President on Summer Riots in 9 Cities over Country," reported in *The New York Times*, September 27, 1964, p. 82.
[2] E. J. Hobsbawm, *Primitive Rebels: Studies in Archaic Forms of Social Movement in the 19th and 20th Centuries* (New York: W. W. Norton and Company, 1959).

[3] Kenneth B. Clark, *Dark Ghetto: Dilemmas of Social Power* (New York: Harper and Row, 1965), pp. 15–16.
[4] On Watts, see Bureau of Criminal Statistics, Department of Justice, State of California, *Watts Riot Arrests, Los Angeles, August 1965* (Sacramento: Bureau of Criminal Statistics, 1966); Raymond J. Murphey and James M. Watson, *The Structure of Discontent: The Relationship Between Social Structure, Grievance, and Support for the Los Angeles Riot* (Los Angeles: University of California, Institute of Government and Public Affairs, 1967). On Detroit, see Irving J. Rubin, "Analyzing Detroit's Riot: The Causes and Responses," *The Reporter*, XXXVIII (February 22, 1968), pp. 34–35. See also Louis H. Masotti and Don R. Bowen, eds., *Riots and Rebellion: Civil Violence in the Urban Community* (Beverly Hills: Sage Publications, 1968).

formed about politics than Negroes who were not involved in the riots. He is more likely to be actively engaged in civil rights efforts, but is extremely distrustful of the political system and of efforts of political leaders."[5]

The riots bore similarities to classical revolutions in which the majority of the participants were neither the criminal elements nor the unemployed or unemployable, but lower-middle-class aspirants with unsatiated wants. Ghetto blacks in revolt were tired of being discriminated against and were fully aware of just how prejudicial their treatment by white society had been. Alienated from the kind of political participation engaged in by some whites and even a few Negroes, they were, nonetheless, politically aware enough to strike out and attract the attention of local and national authorities whom they perceived as being disinterested, at best, or sadistically delighted, at worst, in their plight. The hopelessness and frustration which they found in the ghetto was seen in contrast to the white world outside; and it was to this latter world that they aspired.

II

Small incidents start the riots, but basic causes are deeper and more complex. People living in Watts, Harlem, and the ghettos of Chicago, Detroit, Baltimore, Washington and other large urban areas have spent years living with frustration. Those who have come North from Southern towns have faced unfulfilled expectations, for Northern ghettos did not turn out to be the milk and honey paradises imagined from the vantage point of a rural, impoverished South Carolina town. Impersonal city life is cold and confusing to a youth raised in the folkways and the mores of a Black Belt farm.

Those born in the Northern ghettos and brought up amidst their squalor are also dissatisfied. Television and radio, taking their cues from the sophisticates of Madison Avenue, project images of affluence which produce desires incapable of being fulfilled by the money which blacks have left over at the end of the month. Negroes, as recipients of media messages, are convinced that they need the storehouse of goods which white America has to offer; but the mere demand for an object is not sufficient to bring about its peaceful delivery. Conditioned, in reflex terms, to wanting what the society puts up for sale, the ghetto dweller sees goods and wants them—feels that he needs them if he is to be a man and if he is to have and be a part of the American way of life. He seeks "to share in both the material resources of our system and and its intangible benefits—dignity, respect and acceptance."[6] Wanting but not being able to have, he rationalizes and becomes apathetic, submissive, and compliant or directs his energies into hate, defiance, or rebellion. White America defines success, defines worth and manhood, defines the breed of the elect; but because of a variety of historical and psychological factors, all of which are interrelated, these definitions do not come easy to the black American.

For many people in the ghetto, there is no work; for others, there is only low pay for menial work. There is poverty and hunger, economic exploitation and substandard living, high morbidity, high mortality, and high crime levels. Homes are overcrowded, old and dilapidated, family life unstable, children poorly educated. To quote from the Riot Commission *Report:*

Negro median family income was only 58 percent of the white median income in 1966.[7]

. . . unemployment rates for Negroes are still double those for whites. . . .[8]

. . . a high proportion of the persons living in these areas [low income neighborhoods of nine large cities] were "underemployed," that is they were either

[5] National Advisory Commission on Civil Disorders, *Report of the National Advisory Commission on Civil Disorders* (New York: Bantam Books, 1968), p. 129. See also the *Supplementary Studies for the National Advisory Commission on Civil Disorders* (Washington: U.S. Government Printing Office, 1968).

[6] *Report of the National Advisory Commission on Civil Disorders, op. cit.,* p. 204.
[7] *Ibid.,* p. 251.
[8] *Ibid.,* p. 253.

part-time workers looking for full-time employment, or full-time workers earning less than $3000 per year, or had dropped out of the labor force.[9]

. . . about 11.9 percent of the nation's whites and about 40.6 percent of its nonwhites were poor under the Social Security definition. . . . The poor whites were much older on the average than the poor nonwhites. The proportion of poor persons 65 years old or older was 23.2 percent among the whites but only 6.8 percent among nonwhites.[10]

In the ghettos of many large cities, illegitimacy rates exceed 50 percent."[11]

Of the 59,720 addicts known to the U.S. Bureau of Narcotics at the end of 1966, just over 50 percent were Negroes.[12]

Both income and race appear to affect crime rates: the lower the income in an area, the higher the crime rate there. Yet low-income Negro areas have significantly higher crime rates than low-income white areas. This reflects the high degree of social disorganization in Negro areas . . . as well as the fact that poor Negroes, as a group, have lower incomes than poor whites, as a group.[13]

Maternal mortality rates for non-white mothers are four times as high as those for white mothers. . . . Infant mortality rates among non-white babies are 58 percent higher than among whites for those under one month old, and almost three times as high among those from one month to one year old . . . life expectancy at birth was 6.9 years longer for whites (71.0 years) than for nonwhites (64.1 years). . . .[14]

The analyst must not handle these figures as mere statistics. They are the social reality of the ghetto resident, and until that is understood the riots will not be understood. But the ghetto world also exposes a world outside—the world of white, affluent America. On the television screens, which the *Report* calls the "universal appliance,"[15] are the pretty whites, the successful white business-

man, the smiling blond men on the make, the shining autos, the rich, thick minks, the new stereo sets—the wants of America. The media message gives the consciousness of an alternative to black poverty; and in so doing, it is a contributing factor to black demands for their share of white wealth.

The ghetto life into which a black baby is born has certain sociocultural patterns which he is taught to understand and accept: poverty, death, violence, anger, apathy, alienation. He comes to behave as the ghetto world would have him behave, to come to terms with his environment; but his acceptance is linked to a knowledge of white society, to a culture other than his own. The knowledge of the other world makes him hunger after tools, clothes, and material possessions found in that outside culture. Others have more of what he has and much of what he lacks—more in terms of goods, and, linked to this, a social position more exalted than his. It matters little that relative to the poor in other countries poor blacks here are well–off, for American Negroes orient themselves to white reference groups which they regard as successful benefactors of society's affluence. They do not measure themselves down to the poverty-stricken colored groups in India, Bolivia or Nigeria. Relative deprivation, not absolute deprivation, operates to create feelings of frustration. For how does a ghetto black reconcile the high aspirations which are encouraged by American culture and its achievement ethic and the fact that he cannot legally actualize such aspirations? Either he must admit that he has failed by his own lack of accomplishment or argue that the system is rigged against him. Others—those outside the ghetto or those within it who are perceived as "white niggers" because of their likeness to those outside—have defined what is good and what is right. Until such time as they no longer have the power to define, the Negro is taught to aspire to their standards if he is to get the rewards which the system has to offer. And American culture rewards

[9] *Ibid.*, p. 257.
[10] *Ibid.*, pp. 258–259.
[11] *Ibid.*, p. 262.
[12] *Ibid.*, p. 263.
[13] *Ibid.*, p. 267.
[14] *Ibid.*, p. 270.
[15] *Ibid.*, p. 204.

those who "do," since it measures a
man's worth by his work. In the words
of the Riot Commission *Report:* "The capacity to obtain and hold a 'good job' is
the traditional test of participation in
American society. Steady employment
with adequate compensation provides
both the purchasing power and social
status. It develops the capabilities, confidence, and self-esteem an individual
needs to be a responsible citizen and
provide a basis for a stable family life."[16]
Jobs give money, and money gives the
material goods by which we measure
how worthy we are, how worthy others
think we are, and how stable and committed we need to be.

A Negro knows what the socially approved values of white culture are: his
family, his school, his church, his television (especially his television) tell him
of the social heritage which he is at one
and the same time barred from and
taught to aspire to. He also sees the violence of the ghetto, the violence used
by white authorities against Negroes,
and the force used by the armed
strength of the United States to achieve
its objectives in Vietnam, in the Domini-
can Republic, in Cuba. He is no stranger
to blood and to the idea that might
makes right. Violence for him has become legitimate, a "condition . . . reinforced by a general erosion of respect
for authority in American society. . . ."[17]

Forced to live in two conflicting
worlds, the Negro acts and reflects the
crisis in rules and rituals. If these two
worlds were considered different but
equal, there might be no discord; but
there is an assumed superiority of one
over the other, an imposed hierarchy of
relationships which, although not natural, are culturally-conditioned, socially
approved, and politically institutionalized. Negroes want but cannot seem to
have white materialism—that which is
considered worthy. Until such time as
the cultural artifact of material success
has been devalued or declared unques-
tionable, obsolescent, outmoded, or ir-

relevant, or until such time as the socio-
political world of white America fully
integrates the blacks, Negroes will feel
pressured into continuing to use the
existing channels which are socially dis-
approved or into finding new ones which
bring the desired results.

The riots need to be understood
against this background and seen as a
form of political agitation—a style of
politics. From the perspective of the
ghetto dweller, who wants to integrate
into affluence, the argument can be
made for a reformist movement, one
which accepts the industrial order and
its concomitant values as being valid
and legitimate, but in need of improvement. One need not argue that riots are
part of a revolutionary movement, seeking to radically and fundamentally
transform the present set of social and
political arrangements. Riots are tactics
of social change (which have, of course,
the potential to be counterproductive
as all political tactics do) and can be
equally a part of a strategy which seeks
adjustments in the political order or of
a strategy which wants to qualitatively
change institutions in the civil society.
In the present situation, riots are similar to democratic elections—a tactic to
win an immediate political gain without changing the larger, cultural environment of which the political institutions are but mere parts. But like such
elections, they are signals for action,
not programs or panaceas.

III

To the degree that Negroes are to be
integrated into the industrial arrangements which presently govern economic
and social life, the problem is one of
the price and feasibility of meeting black
demands for material affluence and dignified, equal treatment with white people. As such, it is a question of a technical kind—in the language of the day,
of cost-calculation. This does not mean
that its answer will be immediate and
direct. But the answers to technical
questions are raised without any discussion about the ultimate purposes or
cognitive maps of the society and are,

[16] *Ibid.,* p. 252.
[17] *Ibid.,* p. 205.

therefore, of a kind that require mental changes of a much less grand and sweeping nature than would be the case should the ideology of the social order be held up for criticism.

The Riot Commission is ideal-typical in its technical, reformist response to the outbreaks in the ghetto, offering a series of incremental measures which would integrate blacks into the existing social framework and which would "undertake new initiatives and experiments that can change the system of failure and frustration that now dominates the ghetto and weakens our society."[18] Similarly, many of the large corporations —Ford and Chase Manhattan, to cite but two—are also backing programs which will bring more slum dwellers into the corporate economy, for they are astute enough to equate a stable social order (one in which people have jobs which commit them to the status quo) with safe, rising profits. Similarly, the Nixon proposals for "black capitalism" and the Kennedy proposals for government aid to businesses operating in ghetto areas will bring Negroes into the system on white America's terms; the achievement ethic of the dominant Protestant mentality still remains as the criterion for defining success and individual worth.

In so far as the civil rights or Black Power movement is a form of ethnic politics, it is a handmaiden to the Riot Commission *Report* and to similar integrative proposals. Where Black Power seeks to create images of black as beautiful, and where it seeks to erase the Negro stereotype as wicked, shiftless, lazy, evil, sexually obsessed, and biologically endowed with sexual potency, it is an integrative mechanism. As expounded by the Black Muslims and even some of the leadership of CORE, Black Power is puritanical—a plea for the displacement of erotic potentialities onto one's work, not onto one's play. Black Power, by and large, seeks to picture the Negro as worthy of success in American society as that society would be if her charter values of freedom and equality,

which the proponents of Black Power conceive of as capable of operating within the corporate industrial framework, were to be made real in spirit and real in letter. Blacks will be integrated into American society by making themselves over into the image of those whites in the society who have "made it," who have prestige, power and influence. While, on the one hand, Black Power will solidify and organize blacks on the basis of their shared interests and their blackness, it will, on the other hand, work to melt this blackness into a larger entity—the American Man. The ghettos will be mobilized in terms of group patronage. Representatives of the Negroes will so organize and control Negro communities that they will be able to influence the behavior of the white power-holders, for they will be in a position to negotiate the wishes and demands of a now-disorganized people. Black Power, like other ethnic power movements, presupposes a pluralistic society where groups organized on the basis of certain shared qualities can participate in aggressive political and economic competition. It also presupposes the possibility of changing the environment as soon as the Negro community becomes a power bloc and bringing about meaningful measures of social reform by sticking together and forcing demands upon the power holders. But just as other ethnics have had to become "Americanized," blacks will also have to become Protestant, achievement-and work-oriented, rational, manipulative, calculating and objects of controlled capitalist labor.

It could be argued that Black Power departs from ethnic politics to the extent that it demands control over the ghetto domains, over those urban and rural institutions which affect the lives of ghetto residents—the schools, the police, the businesses, the homes, the social services. However, these cohesive Negro communities, where institutions are responsible to the people over whom they have control, will only be romantic, anachronistic oases in the industrial desert. They may do for the making of dashikis, but they will not build cars, refrigera-

[18] *Ibid.*, p. 2.

tors, or electrical equipment. In and of themselves they are no guarantee of quality teachers or television programs, purified city air, peace in Vietnam, and an end to the arms race—and these are the most important problems that face the American political system today. At best, Negroes in control of isolated communities will be the Black Amish, whom tourists will think of as "quaint" and about whom some white radicals will romanticize as the carriers of social change and the agents for revolutionary rhetoric. At worst, dashikis and Swahili will be but the outer garments of an absorbed, contained, integrated black mass man.

Only when the concept of Black Power turns to a humanism now regarded as antiquated by the larger culture, will it place road-blocs in the path of Negro co-option. Cleaver is a revolutionary when he calls for a reconciliation of the white mind and the black body —the drafting of a bargain whereby "whites have . . . to turn to the blacks for a clue on how to swing with the Body, while the blacks have . . . to turn to the whites for the secret of the Mind"[19]—for here is a call for a qualitative change in social arrangements. Mailer is a revolutionary when he demands that, in spirit, blacks "find a way to educate their own out of textbooks not yet written . . . [and] grapple . . . with the incommensurable problem of policing one's own society . . . explore Black medicine, herbs in place of antibiotics, witchcraft for cancer cures, surgical grace with the knife in preference to heart transfers . . . black notions of labor, cooperation, and the viability of hip in production methods; not housing projects, but a new way to build houses; not shuttle planes, but gliders; not computers—rather psychic induction."[20] Black Power is revolutionary when it is Baldwin's rejection of "that American system which makes pawns of white men and victims of black men and which really, at bottom, considers all artistic effort to be either irrelevant or threatening."[21] It is revolutionary when it rejects a profit system in which people, like things, are properties and when it bares its creative potential for sensuality and the eventual liberation of all black and whites living in the repressive environment of the advanced, industrial society.[22]

Black Power has the potential for becoming a revolutionary ideology to the degree that it negates integrationism and ethnic politics with a black culture and a black consciousness, so that a synthesis is a blend of the technical advances of Western civilization with an ultimate concern for the human being, for the body of that human being, for the bodies of other human beings, for their dignity and their freedom. The black American, if he is to be revolutionary, must do what Senghor demands of the Negro African: that he lead the revolt against materialism; that he reintegrate into the new synthesis the moral values of the African and the political and economic contributions of the revolutions of 1789 and 1917; that he emphasize confrontation and intuition by fusing subject and object, by touching and feeling and smelling objects, by replacing the reason of the eye with the reason of the touch and the embrace.[23]

Blacks have been defined by whites as the other; and, in situational terms, they can use their defined differences to oppose those characteristics which make whites the men of power. They can translate their consciousness of being different into political action by defining white characteristics as those which must no longer be enshrined. No longer content with what whites would have them be, they must become what black conscious-

[19] Eldridge Cleaver, *Soul on Ice* (New York: McGraw-Hill Book Company, 1968), pp. 192–193.
[20] Norman Mailer, "Black Power: A Discussion," *Partisan Review*, Vol. XXXV (Spring 1968), p. 220.
[21] James Baldwin, "The Price May Be Too High," *The New York Times*, February 2, 1969, p. 9.
[22] Herbert Marcuse, *One Dimensional Man: Studies in the Ideology of Advanced Industrial Society* (Boston: Beacon Press, 1964), pp. 256–257.
[23] Léopold Sédar Senghor, *On African Socialism*, trans. Mercer Cook (New York: Frederick A. Prager, 1964).

ness demands they become. Only then do they transcend their white-assigned situation. Men are historical—capable of being other than they are at a given moment; that is, they are capable of self-definition.

Black consciousness, to be defined as revolutionary, must identify with a black heritage and a black reality—a heritage of slavery and oppression, a social world unique to a ghetto subculture. It is a subculture of love and sex, of song and sport, of music and dance, of emotive religions, of slang. It is a world of touch, sound, and feel. But it is also an experience of suffering, of poverty, of crime, and of violence.

At the present time, when the Baldwins and the Cleavers speak against integrating Negroes into an American middle-class, bourgeois with its values that are crass and materialistic, they are appealing more to a few white, middle-class alienates then to ghetto blacks. The socialization processes and the material rewards of affluent America are appealing enough to make those who are out to want in. It is only those who have known the barrenness of being "in" who are prepared to reject, only those who have the cars who want to sell them, only those who have the suburban homes who want to drop-out to a small farm existence, only those who have the social wherewithal to make it in the present system who want to make it on their own terms. To argue that the answers to the good life may not be in gold coin and green power, one must have had that coin and that power to begin with.

In summary, the black revolt has to be seen on two levels. First, its actions to date have been to demand an alteration to the rules and regulations of the democratic corporate state; second, it has the potential for calling into question the very values or legitimate ends of the civil or social order. On one level, it will bring about political reform and on the other, cultural revolution. Lest we forget, there is a qualitative difference between the democratization of the political apparatus and a redefinition of what is good, true, and beautiful—the consciousness of an alternative existence.

Suggestions for Additional Reading

For works of background interest, from which one can understand the present decade in its historical perspective, see Gunnar Myrdal's classic statement on inequality, *An American Dilemma: The Negro Problem and Modern Democracy* (New York: Harper and Brothers, 1944). In the twentieth anniversary edition (1963), there is a new preface by Myrdal and an epilogue by Arnold Rose, who worked closely with Myrdal on the earlier work. For similar scope and durability through these changing years, one should refer to E. Franklin Frazier's *The Negro in the United States*, rev. ed. (New York: Macmillan and Company, 1957). For a specifically Southern perspective, see W. J. Cash, *The Mind of the South* (New York: Alfred A. Knopf, 1941); John Dollard, *Caste and Class in a Southern Town*, 3rd ed. (New York: Yale University Press, 1957); Erskine Caldwell, *In Search of Bisco* (New York: Farrar, Straus and Giroux, 1965); and C. Vann Woodward, *The Burden of Southern History* (Baton Rouge: Louisiana State University Press, 1960). For a classic study of black urban life, see St. Clair Drake and Horace R. Clayton, *Black Metropolis: A Study of Negro Life in a Northern City*, rev. ed. (New York: Harper and Row, 1963); Nathan Glazer and Daniel Patrick Moynihan, *Beyond the Melting Pot: The Negroes, Puerto Ricans, Jewish, Italians and Irish of New York City* (Cambridge: M.I.T. Press and Harvard University Press, 1963); and Kenneth B. Clark, *Dark Ghetto: Dilemmas of Social Power* (New York: Harper and Row, 1965). And for its historical comprehensiveness, see John Hope Franklin, *From Slavery to Freedom: A History of American Negroes,* 2nd ed. (New York: Alfred A. Knopf, 1956).

For contemporary overviews, see Talcott Parsons and Kenneth B. Clark, eds., *The Negro American* (Boston: Beacon Press, 1965). Of particular relevance in that collection are the essays by St. Clair Drake, "The Social and Economic Status of the Negro in the United States"; Rashi Fein, "An Economic and Social Profile of the Negro American"; Erik H. Erikson, "The Concept of Identity in Race Relations: Notes and Queries"; James Q. Wilson, "The Negro in Politics"; Kenneth B. Clark, "The Civil Rights Movement: Momentum and Organization"; and John B. Turner and Whitney M. Young, Jr., "Who Has the Revolution or Thoughts on the Second Reconstruction." For another succinct overview, see Charles E. Silberman, *Crisis in Black and White* (New York: Random House, 1964).

On the civil rights movement itself, the mood is set in James Baldwin's *The Fire Next Time* (New York: Dial Press, 1963). The various strands of the movement are laid out and analyzed in Nat Hentoff's *The New Equality* (New York: Viking Press, 1964); Lewis M. Killian's *The Impossible Revolution? Black Power and the American Dream* (New York: Random House, 1968); Martin Luther King, Jr., *Where Do We Go From Here: Chaos or Community* (Boston: Beacon Press, 1967); and Julius Lester's, *Look Out, Whitey! Black Power's Gon' Get Your Mama!* (New York: Dial Press, 1968).

A young classic which sets out the case for coalition politics, to which the responses are still coming in, is Bayard Rustin's "From Protest to Politics: The Future of the Civil Rights Movement," *Commentary*, XXXIX (February 1965), 25–31. For a similar view, see Tom Kahn, "Problems of the Negro Movement: A Special Report," *Dissent*, XI (Winter 1964), 108–138. For a dissenting view, see Ronald Radosh, "From Protest to Black Power: The Failure of Coalition Politics," in *The Great Society Reader: The Failure of American Liberalism*, eds., Marvin E. Gettleman and David Mermelstein (New York: Random House, 1967), pp. 278–293. For the militant perspective, see James Boggs, *The American Revolution: Pages from a Negro Worker's Notebook* (New York: Monthly Review Press, 1963) and Robert Williams, *Negroes with Guns* (New York: Marzani and Munsell, 1964).

For an overview of the economic conditions of blacks in America, see Peter M. Blau and Otis Dudley Duncan, *The American Occuptional Structure* (New York: John Wiley and Sons, 1967) and Louis A. Ferman et al., eds., *Negroes and Jobs: A Book of Readings* (Ann Arbor: University of Michigan Press, 1968). Specifically on the poor black, see Michael Harrington's significant work which has been credited with instigating the government's attack on poverty, *The Other America: Poverty in the United States* (Baltimore: Penguin Books, 1963). Also see Ben H. Bagdikian, *In the Midst of Plenty: The Poor in America* (Boston: Beacon Press, 1964); Louis A. Ferman et al., eds., *Poverty in America* (Ann Arbor: University of Michigan Press, 1965); and Gunnar Myrdal, *Challenge of Affluence* (New York: Pantheon Books, 1964).

Related to these conditions, much has been written on the black family as a social institution. Lee Rainwater and William L. Yancy in *The Moynihan Report and the Politics of Controversy* (Cambridge: M.I.T. Press, 1967) collect the debate on the cultures of poverty, their political implications, and the economic consequences of black family breakdown. For an earlier view, see E. Franklin Frazier's *The Negro Family*

in the United States, rev. ed. (Chicago University of Chicago Press, 1966) and on the black middle class, his *Blacl Bourgeoisie,* rev. ed. (New York: Collie Books, 1962).

In so far as black politics is con cerned, see Edward C. Banfield and James Q. Wilson, *City Politics* (Cam bridge: Harvard University Press, 1963) for its analysis of why blacks operate less through the political machines and more in the courts and/or streets. Ref erence should also be made to James Q Wilson, *Negro Politics: The Search fo Leadership* (Glencoe: Free Press, 1960) On ethnic politics in general, see Rober E. Lane, *Political Life: Why and Hou People Get Involved in Politics* (Glen coe: Free Press, 1959). For a behaviora analysis of such involvement, see Wil liam Brink and Louis Harris, *The Ne gro Revolution in America* (New York Simon and Schuster, 1967); Gary T Marx, *Protest and Prejudice: A Study o Belief in the Black Community* (Nev York: Harper and Row, 1967); and Don ald R. Matthews and James W. Prothro *Negroes and the New Southern Politics* (New York: Harcourt, Brace and World 1966).

A very good collection of articles or riots and violence is to be found in Louis H. Masotti and Don R. Bowen, eds., *Ri ots and Rebellion: Civil Violence in the Urban Community* (Beverly Hills: Sage Publications, 1968). In particular, ref erence should be made to the editors "Civil Violence: A Theoretical Over view"; James H. Laue, "Power, Conflict and Social Change"; Allen D. Grim shaw, "Three Views of Urban Violence Civil Disturbance, Racial Revolt, Class Assault"; E. L. Quarantelli and Russel Dynes, "Looting in Civil Disorders: An Index of Social Change"; and H. L. Nie burg, "Violence, Law and the Socia Process." Another series of intelligen and informed articles is edited by Rob ert H. Connery, "Urban Riots: Violence and Social Change," *Proceedings of the Academy of Political Science*, XXIX (1968), 1–190. Of import are the essays by Barrington Moore, Jr., "Thoughts or Violence and Democracy"; St. Clai

Drake, "Urban Violence and American Social Movements"; Robert M. Fogelson, "Violence as Protest"; and Bruce L. R. Smith, "The Politics of Protest: How Effective Is Violence?" In this connection, see also Hannah Arendt, "Reflections on Violence," *Journal of International Affairs*, XXIII (1969), 1–35; Franz Schurmann, "On Revolutionary Conflict," *ibid.*, 36–53; and Charles V. Hamilton, "Conflict, Race and System-Transformation in the United States," *ibid.*, 106–118. Three books on this subject that should also be consulted are: Arthur I. Waskow, *From Race Riots to Sit-ins, 1919 and the 1960's: A Study in the Connections Between Conflict and Violence* (Garden City: Doubleday and Company, 1966); Tom Hayden, *Rebellion in Newark: Official Violence and Ghetto Response* (New York: Random House, 1967); and Hugh Davis Graham and Tedd Robert Gurr, eds., *Violence in America: Historical and Comparative Perspectives: A Report Submitted to the National Commission on the Causes and Prevention of Violence* (New York: Bantam Books, 1969). For a more polemical perspective, see Robert F. Williams, *Negroes with Guns* (New York: Marzani and Munsell, 1962) and Truman Nelson, *The Right of Revolution* (Boston: Beacon Press, 1968).

For general works on the background of Black Power, see Floyd Barbour, ed., *The Black Power Revolt: A Collection of Essays* (Boston: Porter Sargeant, 1968); Robert Coles et al., "Black Power: A Discussion," *Partisan Review*, XXXV (Spring 1968), 195–232; and Martin Duberman, "Black Power and the American Radical Tradition," *Partisan Review*, XXXV (Winter 1968), 34–68, which provoked the preceding discussion. On the Black Muslims, see E. U. Essien-Udom, *Black Nationalism: A Search for an Identity in America* (Chicago: University of Chicago Press, 1962) and C. Eric Lincoln, *Black Muslims in America* (Boston: Beacon Press, 1961). Other general analyses are to be found in Stokely Carmichael's "Toward Black Liberation," *Massachusetts Review*, VII (Autumn 1966), 639–665 and his "What

We Want," *New York Review of Books*, IX (September 22, 1966), 5–6, 8; Harold Cruse's *The Crisis of the Negro Intellectual* (New York: William Morrow and Company, 1967) and his *Rebellion or Revolution?* (New York: William Morrow and Company, 1968).

Specifically, on the discussion of the utilization of Black Power for political purposes, see Stokely Carmichael and Charles V. Hamilton, *Black Power: The Politics of Liberation in America* (New York: Random House, 1967); Charles V. Hamilton, "An Advocate of Black Power Defines It," *New York Times*, April 14, 1968, pp. 22–23, 79–83; Bayard Rustin, " 'Black Power' and Coalition Politics," *Commentary*, XLII (September 1966), 35–40; Paul Feldman's "How the Cry for 'Black Power' Began," *Dissent*, XIII (September–October, 1966), 472–77 and his "The Pathos of 'Black Power,' " *Dissent*, XIV (January–February 1967), 69–79; David Danzig, "In Defense of 'Black Power,' " *Commentary*, XLII (September 1966), 41–46; and Christopher Lasch, "A Special Supplement: The Trouble with Black Power," *New York Review of Books*, X (February 29, 1968), 4–14.

For works on Black Power which deal with the psychological perspective, see Eldridge Cleaver, *Soul on Ice* (New York: McGraw-Hill Book Company, 1968); Malcolm X, The Autobiography of Malcolm X (New York: Grove Press, 1964); George Breitman, ed., *Malcolm X Speaks: Selected Speeches and Statements* (New York: Grove Press, 1966); and Frantz Fanon, *The Wretched of the Earth* (New York: Grove Press, 1963).

The black personality is dealt with in William H. Grier and Price M. Cobbs, *Black Rage* (New York: Basic Books, 1968), which is but another thematic treatment of the aggression-frustration thesis dealt with in Abram Kardiner and Lionel Ovesey, *The Mark of Oppression: Explorations in the Personality of the American Negro* (Cleveland: World Publishing Company) and in Alfred F. Poussaint, "A Negro Psychiatrist Explains the Negro Psyche," *The New York Times*, August 20, 1967, pp. 52–

53, 55–56, 58, 73, 75–76, 78, 80. In this connection, see also Robert Coles, *Children of Crisis: A Study of Courage and Fear* (Boston: Little, Brown and Company, 1967).

For the elucidation of the sexuality thesis, see the writings of James Baldwin, especially *Giovanni's Room* (New York: Dial Press, 1956), *Another Country* (New York: Dial Press, 1962), and *Blues for Mister Charlie* (New York: Dial Press, 1964). Norman Mailer's treatment of "Minorities" in *The Presidential Papers* (New York: Bantam Books, 1964) and "The White Negro" in *Advertisements for Myself* (New York: Bantam Books, 1959) reiterate the Negritude thesis. On this subject, see also Jean Genet, *The Blacks: A Clown Show,* trans. Bernard Frechtman (New York: Grove Press, 1961) and Robert Gover, *One Hundred Dollar Misunderstanding* (New York: Ballantine Books, 1963). A socio-psychological treatment is found in Calvin C. Hernton, *Sex and Racism in America* (New York: Grove Press, 1965).

For the argument which rejects a uniquely black culture, see Hylan Lewis, *Blackways of Kent* (Chapel Hill: University of North Carolina Press, 1955). An opposing viewpoint, in which the argument is made that blacks have a perspective or view of reality, that arises from and relates to their black situation, see Charles Keil, *Urban Blues* (Chicago: University of Chicago Press, 1966) and Leroi Jones, *Black Music* (New York: William Morrow and Company, 1968).

On a larger perspective, a total view of the social reality against which the civil rights and black power struggles have to be seen, understood, and evaluated, see the National Advisory Commission on Civil Disorders, *Report of the National Advisory Commission on Civil Disorders-* (Washington: U.S. Government Printing Office, 1968). A more theoretical perspective of American society, but one which has to be grappled with if the problem of political dissent is to be understood, is Herbert Marcuse's *One Dimensional Man: Studies in the Ideology of Advanced Industrial Society* (Boston: Beacon Press, 1964). Supplementary to the latter are: Lewis A. Coser, *Continuities in the Study of Social Conflict* (New York: Free Press, 1967); Chalmers Johnson, *Revolutionary Change* (Boston: Little, Brown and Company, 1966); Mitchell Cohen and Dennis Hale, eds., *The New Student Left: An Anthology* (Boston: Beacon Press, 1966); Paul Jacobs and Saul Landau, *The New Radicals: A Report with Documents* (New York: Random House, 1966); and Jack Newfield, *A Prophetic Minority* (New York: New American Library, 1966). Also see Ben B. Seligman's *Most Notorious Victory: Man in an Age of Automation* (New York: Free Press, 1966) and his *Permanent Poverty: An American Syndrome* (Chicago: Quadrangle Books, 1968); Jonathan Kozol, *Death at an Early Age: The Destruction of the Hearts and Minds of Negro Children in the Boston Public Schools* (New York: Bantam Books, 1967); Irving Howe, "New Styles in 'Leftism,'" *Dissent,* XII (Summer 1965), 295–323; and Stephen Spender, *The Year of the Young Rebels* (New York: Random House, 1969).

For a sobering conclusion, one should reflect on the arguments raised in André Gorz, *Strategy for Labor: A Radical Proposal,* trans. Martin A. Nicolaus and Victoria Ortiz (Boston: Beacon Press, 1967) and Herbert Marcuse, *Essay on Liberation* (Boston: Beacon Press, 1969).

DATE DUE

DATE DUE

MAY 2000			
			Printed in USA